insight text guide

Virginia Lee

Fahrenheit 451

Ray Bradbury

First published in 2022, reprinted in 2023, 2024.

Insight Publications Pty Ltd
3/350 Charman Road
Cheltenham VIC 3192
Australia
Tel: +61 3 8571 4950
Email: books@insightpublications.com.au

www.insightpublications.com.au

A catalogue record for this book is available from the National Library of Australia

Ray Bradbury's Fahrenheit 451 / Virginia Lee

Virginia Lee asserts the moral right to be identified as the author of this work.

ISBNs:
9781922525611 (print)
9781922525628 (digital)

Cover design by Gisela Beer

Printed by Markono Print Media Pte Ltd

contents

CHARACTER MAP

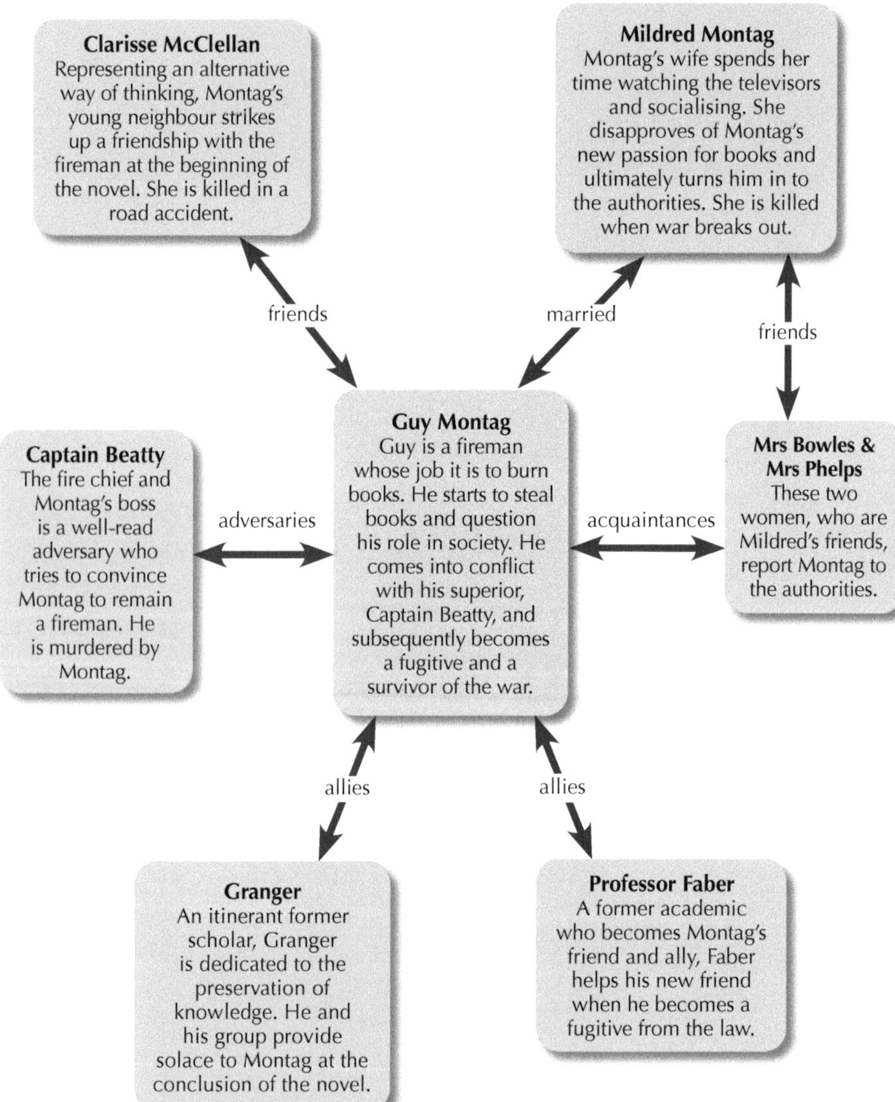

OVERVIEW

About the author

Ray Bradbury (1920–2012) was one of the most influential American writers of his generation. Although he wrote more than fifty works across a variety of genres – including several screenplays for film and television – he is primarily recognised for his contribution to science fiction. *Fahrenheit 451* (1953) remains his best-known novel. Other popular works include his short-story collections, *The Martian Chronicles* (1950) and *The Illustrated Man* (1951), and the coming-of-age novel *Dandelion Wine* (1957). His books have sold more than eight million copies and been translated into more than thirty-six languages.

As a boy, Bradbury was a voracious reader, especially of science fiction. In his introduction to the 50th Anniversary Edition of *Fahrenheit 451* (reproduced in the 2008 edition cited here), he describes himself as someone who had been 'a library person all of [his] life' (p.3). Bradbury started writing his own stories from an early age and, by twenty-four, he was a full-time writer. His work combined an imaginative, ambivalent attitude towards the future with incisive social criticism.

Throughout a long and celebrated career, Bradbury received many accolades. In 2000 he was awarded the Medal for Distinguished Contribution to American Letters from the National Book Foundation and, in 2004, he received the National Medal for the Arts. In 2007, Bradbury received a special citation from the Pulitzer Prize jury 'for his distinguished, prolific and deeply influential career as an unmatched author of science fiction and fantasy' (cited in Jonas 2012).

Many of Bradbury's works have been adapted to film, television and other media. *Fahrenheit 451* was made into two films: a version directed by François Truffaut (1966) and, more recently, a version for HBO directed by Ramin Bahrani (2018).

Synopsis

A future American government keeps its citizens on a tight leash, with repressive controls that forbid them to act as they choose. Reading and possessing books is outlawed and there are severe penalties for breaking the law. Instead of putting fires out, firemen now have a policing role: they raid the homes of those they suspect of harbouring illicit material and systematically destroy these materials. People are kept busy chasing pleasure, and one of the primary forms of entertainment is watching the huge television screens called 'televisors' or 'parlour walls'.

Guy Montag, a fireman, derives great satisfaction from his work. Coming home one evening, he meets a young neighbour, Clarisse McClellan, and strikes up a conversation with her. Clarisse invites Montag to rethink several aspects of his own life, including whether or not he is happy. The subsequent suicide attempt of his wife, Mildred, is a harsh indicator of the emptiness of their life together. Montag starts to question the society in which he lives and his role within it. He feels increasingly disconnected at work, and uncomfortable in the menacing presence of the Mechanical Hound.

Meanwhile, Montag has a guilty secret. He has been stealing books for some time, surreptitiously adding to the small collection hidden behind the ventillator grille in his home. Montag's burgeoning friendship with Clarisse comes to an abrupt conclusion when she is killed in a car accident. Another incident occurs that exacerbates the fireman's disquiet: a woman whose house is being burned refuses to leave, and so dies with her books. Montag is shaken by her stance.

To Mildred's consternation, Montag decides that he does not want to be a fireman any longer. Captain Beatty, anticipating his employee's reluctance, visits the couple and delivers a lecture on the history of book burning. This does not change Montag's mind and he starts to read his own cache of illegal books.

After arguing with his resistant wife, Montag seeks out Professor Faber, whom he had met once before. Faber recognises the government's oppression for what it is, but has been too frightened to resist. He finally agrees to help Montag, giving him a small earpiece through which the fireman can listen to him.

When Montag returns home, Mildred's friends, Mrs Phelps and Mrs Bowles, pay a visit. Infuriated by their shallowness, Montag insists on reading to them from a book of poetry, thus exposing himself as a dissident.

Montag returns to the fire station where Beatty again tries to convince him of his foolishness. Shortly after, an alarm is called in and Montag finds himself outside his own house. Both Mildred and her friends have denounced him.

Mildred flees the scene without a backward glance at her husband. The fire chief rails at Montag as the latter is forced to burn down his own house – an act he finds surprisingly cathartic. Beatty then strikes Montag, knocking Faber's audio-capsule out of his ear. When Beatty threatens to arrest the professor, Montag turns the flamethrower on him. Montag also destroys the Mechanical Hound after it attacks him.

The long-awaited war is finally declared. Now a fugitive, Montag eludes the police and makes his way through the city. As a retaliatory gesture, he plants the few remaining books that he has rescued in the home of a fireman, and rings in the alarm. He visits Faber to say goodbye, giving the old man some money. Faber tells Montag that he is also escaping the city, and advises the fireman to head towards the river.

Montag escapes downriver to the countryside, where he meets a small group of elderly men, led by Granger. They watch Montag's staged death on a portable TV, and Granger explains their mission. They are part of a network committed to memorising the contents of the books that have been lost, metaphorical 'dust-jackets' (p.196). When the time is right, this knowledge will again be available to those who value it.

An atomic bomb destroys the city; the high casualty rate includes Mildred. Soberly, the men head back towards the scene, hoping to help any survivors they may find. Montag leads the way, reciting to himself from the Bible.

Character summaries

Guy Montag

Montag is the protagonist of the novel. He is a thirty-year-old fireman who is married to Mildred. Curious about the books that are banned by his government, Montag becomes disillusioned with the role he has played in destroying these items. He comes into conflict with Captain Beatty and becomes one of a small group of individuals who reject the tyranny of the State.

Mildred Montag

Thirty-year-old Mildred is Montag's wife. She does not work, spending all her time watching her parlour walls and visiting friends. She calls in the alarm on Montag after he brings stolen books into their home.

Clarisse McClellan

Montag's seventeen-year-old neighbour strikes up an unlikely friendship with him, opening his eyes to the unhappiness he feels. Clarisse is killed by a speeding car.

Captain Beatty

The antagonist of the novel, Beatty is the middle-aged fire chief and Montag's boss. Clever and very literate, Beatty realises early on that Montag is having doubts and seeks to persuade him back to his profession as a fireman.

Professor Faber

Faber is a retired English professor. After losing his teaching position when the demand for studying the humanities dried up, Faber became a recluse. He becomes Montag's sole ally.

Granger

Granger is a former librarian and author who became a fugitive after he struck a fireman for burning his library. He now travels the countryside with a small group of fellow academics who keep the knowledge from books safely in their heads.

Mrs Phelps

Mrs (Clara) Phelps is one of Mildred's friends. She is about the same age as Mildred, and is similarly married with no children.

Mrs Bowles

Mrs Bowles is also a friend of Mildred's. She has two children and has outlived three husbands.

Stoneman and Black

Stoneman and Black are firemen who work with Montag.

BACKGROUND & CONTEXT

The United States in the 1950s

Politically, the 1950s was a deeply conservative decade, dominated by the Cold War. This undeclared war of suspicion and espionage between the United States and the Soviet Union shaped US foreign policy and had profound implications for American citizens at home. *Fahrenheit 451* was written within this context, when the threat of nuclear hostilities hovered over the US. The dropping of atomic bombs on Hiroshima and Nagasaki in August 1945 was a relatively recent event, and an attack by the Soviet Union was considered possible, if not imminent. Bradbury re-creates this environment in the novel, with bombers crossing the sky 'every hour' (p.96) as the country prepares for war.

The US entered a period of unprecedented economic prosperity after World War II. It was a time of fiscal growth – driven by a number of factors, including the car industry and a housing boom – and increased consumerism. Employment opportunities were extensive. The new medium of television, underpinned as it was by advertising, proved to be the perfect vehicle through which to promote the many products that were flooding the market. Large corporations expanded their international presence, while new franchises, such as McDonald's, were establishing themselves in the domestic market.

Although set in the future, *Fahrenheit 451* presents a world in which women's roles are as limited as they were in the 1950s. Women of this generation were largely dependent on men, economically and socially; indeed, many women were legally required to give up their jobs when they married. Few women went on to further study after school or had ambitions beyond marriage. The expectation was that they become homemakers and support their husband's career aspirations, irrespective of whether they had children. In the text, Mildred spends her days watching her parlour walls and socialising with her friends, whose husbands 'come and go' on army deployment (p.122).

Fahrenheit 451 is, of course, a product of its times, and reflects the dominant white culture of middle-class America. The civil rights movement was still a decade away; hence, Montag's socially advantaged circle excludes people of colour.

McCarthyism

The deep distrust of the Soviet Union and pervasive fear of communism led to the establishment of several anti-communist government agencies, including the House of Un-American Activities Committee (HUAC). After World War II, this committee intensified its efforts to flush out and vilify those who were deemed a threat to the American way of life. From 1950, Republican senator Joseph McCarthy rose to notoriety as an aggressive campaigner against communism, hunting down individuals with ruthless, almost religious, zeal. Civil liberties were suspended and thousands of Americans were blacklisted as communists or communist sympathisers; many lost their careers, and some even went to prison. As a liberal democrat, Bradbury recoiled from this disturbing agenda – subsequently known as 'McCarthyism' – and, in part, *Fahrenheit 451* was written in response to the political dogma being championed by the conservative right.

The arrival of television

The novel is set well before the advent of home computers, the internet and social media; however, by the early 1950s television had started making its presence felt in American homes and was growing exponentially in popularity. By the end of the decade, approximately fifty-five million households across the US had televisions, with viewers watching programs from over 500 stations. It became the primary medium through which mass audiences accessed entertainment, news, sport and, of course, advertising – a vast platform from which to sell products and personalities. Television's cultural impact was unprecedented. It both played to and manipulated cultural tastes, blurring regional differences and helping to shape a homogenised national popular culture that, in turn, was exported to the rest of the world.

Television's reach was quickly recognised by politicians. Televising debates between presidential candidates became the norm, and this exposure transformed the way in which the message was delivered. Political advertising campaigns began to feature 'sound bites' – short, pithy statements from a candidate – rather than lengthy speeches that threatened to lose audience interest. *Fahrenheit 451* alludes to a political landscape in which substance has become less important than appearance. As Montag's discussion with his wife's friends makes clear, the electorate is more inclined to vote for a candidate who pleases the eye, rather than the ear.

Television attracted its critics from the outset, though. While there were some quality programs, much of what was on offer was banal and pedestrian in the extreme, pandering to the lowest common denominator. The way in which television redefined how people utilised their leisure time and interacted with others was also a source of angst to many. People spent more time at home, watching their favourite programs – they socialised less, exercised less and, arguably, read less. The invasive impact of television and the attendant 'dumbing-down' of literacy concerned Bradbury to such a degree that, in the novel, he presents an exaggerated scenario in which the community's reliance on television has become excessive. Huge wall units are now the preferred form of entertainment in the home. At $2000 a screen – one-third of Montag's annual salary – they are an innovation for the well-off. Designed to entertain and pacify, these parlour walls overwhelm the living space, imposing sensation, but intentionally quashing any opportunity for meaningful discourse.

Book burning

Book burning as a form of censorship has a long and ignominious history. Throughout millennia, it has been adopted by both secular and religious authorities as a means of control – a pre-emptive strategy to quell agitation by discrediting, then desecrating, knowledge. From the book burnings of the Chinese Emperor Qin Shi Huang in 213 BC to the Spanish Inquisition's destruction of 5000 Arabic manuscripts in the late fifteenth century, the practice has stood as a powerful symbol of intolerance and the suppression of ideas.

Bradbury alludes to several examples in his Afterword to *Fahrenheit 451*. A self-professed bibliophile, he was deeply affected when, as a child, he learned about the destruction of the Great Library of Alexandria in Egypt. This library – part of a museum complex founded in the third century BC – was one of the largest and most important institutions of learning in the ancient world; at its height, it was an intellectual hub that housed a collection of up to 400 000 papyrus scrolls.

The library's decline probably occurred over several centuries, starting with an accidental burning by Julius Caesar in 48 BC during a battle with the Egyptians. Subsequently, as a repository of independent scholarship, the library became a provocation to increasingly reactionary Christian powers. In 391 AD, the original structure was destroyed by Theophilus, the Bishop of Alexandria, as part of a campaign to wipe out paganism. A final burning may have occurred in 642 AD when the Arabs – supposedly intolerant of the Christian texts that were now housed in the library – captured Alexandria.

Bradbury also cites the 'rumours of Stalin and his match-people and tinderboxes' (p.221). In Josef Stalin's Soviet Union, books were regarded as instruments of propaganda and those that did not promote socialist dogma were censored rigorously. This resulted in the burning of countless numbers of books that were considered 'decadent' by the communists throughout the 1920s and 1930s, and was part of a broader witch-hunt against creative writers, intellectuals and academics.

Bradbury's own generation was familiar with the infamous book burnings of the Nazis during the 1930s. After the National Socialists came to power in Germany in 1933, they quickly instigated a purge against books and writers they deemed 'un-German'. Under the direction of Joseph Goebbels – Minister for Public Enlightenment and Propaganda – the stated aim was to homogenise German culture and bring all aspects of the arts in line with Nazi ideology.

Across the country, the fascist German Student Union created blacklists of works by prominent Jewish, liberal and leftist authors, such as Sigmund Freud, Karl Marx, Bertolt Brecht and Erich Maria Remarque. From 10 May 1933, coordinated book burnings were carried out by university students in thirty-four German towns and cities. Subsequently, the Nazis raided bookshops and libraries to confiscate and destroy books considered to be subversive or dangerous. The book burnings were condemned internationally as being incompatible with a modern, civilised society, and pointed to the sinister agenda that was to follow.

GENRE, STRUCTURE & LANGUAGE

Genre

Fahrenheit 451 is a dystopian novel. It shows a frightening future in which the American people have abolished democratic rights and intellectual independence in favour of a hedonistic lifestyle. The exact time is unspecified, though it is clear that the text is set in the United States, post-1960.

Like all good speculative fiction, *Fahrenheit 451* identifies and builds on current political and social trends in order to predict a scenario in which events are played out to a plausible conclusion. In this sense, the novel is also an allegory. Both a critique and a warning, it offers a worrying appraisal of the US in the early 1950s, and the public's apparent collusion in its own demise. In Bradbury's parable, American prosperity has led to societal complacency; the development of atomic weaponry and the aggressive arms race with the Soviet Union has led to a globally hostile US; and overreach on the part of authorities – particularly in relation to so-called communist activities – has led to the emergence of a police state.

With the advent of television, Bradbury was highly critical of mass media, which he held responsible for declining literacy standards. In the text, the last liberal arts college was shut down forty years before the story commences, caused by the lack of students and funding. *Fahrenheit 451* also foresees a post-truth world in which facts are manipulated, misinformation disseminated and history rewritten. The novel is particularly relevant in the age of social media. Written before the internet revolutionised society, it nevertheless anticipates the potentially invasive nature of technology and the way in which it can come to dominate people's lives.

Structure

The novel has a conventional linear structure and is set over a period of less than a week. The narrative is divided into three sections: 'The Hearth and the Salamander', 'The Sieve and the Sand' and 'Burning Bright'. These headings figuratively represent the progressive stages in Montag's journey towards spiritual freedom: from unquestioning servant of the State to outcast and insurgent.

The hearth and the salamander represent the twin aspects of fire – its life-giving properties, as well as its ability to destroy. This imagery speaks to humanity's ambivalent relationship with fire, which can be both comforting and terrifying: 'He had never thought in his life that it could give as well as take' (p.187).

These symbols also represent the twin aspects of Montag's identity: husband and fireman. The hearth, or fireplace, is the traditional symbol of the home, of comfort, security and refuge. However, one of the chilling features of Montag's life – and this becomes increasingly obvious to him – is that his home does *not* provide comfort of any sort. The other aspect of Montag's life is his work, the emblem of which is the salamander. In legend, salamanders were lizard-like creatures that possessed an affinity with fire; in Montag's world, the iconography representing fire is ubiquitous, emblazoned on everything from his lighter to the fire truck.

The title of the second section evokes a boyhood memory at the beach in which Montag attempts to fill a sieve with sand. The impossibility of the task is akin to memorising the information contained in the Bible he has stolen. Yet Montag is starting to understand the value of what has been denied to society by the State, and he is compelled to question his own role in championing its cause.

The final section references William Blake's poem 'The Tyger', from *Songs of Innocence and Experience*. Blake's tiger, forged in the fire of a transcendent imagination, evokes both beauty and terror, its creator inciting awe as well as admiration for his daring. The tiger, burning so brightly, symbolises the divine incentive within the human soul that enables humankind to resist social oppression and other evils associated with the corrupt world of experience. Montag is an imperfect, yet ultimately worthy, exponent of this striving.

Language

Polemical in intent and didactic in tone, *Fahrenheit 451* is passionate in terms of conveying its message. Consequently, dialogue, bordering on speechmaking, features prominently in the text, as several characters declare their views for Montag's benefit. Chief Beatty and Professor Faber each deliver their arguments in lengthy monologues that represent opposing sides of the debate. Bradbury's own audience is, of course, also invited to consider the arguments, and both Montag and the readers must choose between these: 'All right, he's had his say ... I'll say my say, too ... And you'll try to judge them and make your decision as to which way to jump, or fall' (p.140).

Bradbury writes in lyrical, expressive prose and his extensive use of metaphor is an arresting feature of the text. In particular, images of fire and burning predominate. Reflecting on his first conversation with Clarisse, Montag feels his smile slip away, 'melt, fold over, and down on itself like a tallow skin, like the stuff of a fantastic candle burning too long and now collapsing and now blown out' (pp.19–20). Mildred's friends, shallow and anti-intellectual, have 'Cheshire Cat smiles' (p.121) that 'burn' through the walls of the house.

Throughout the text, Bradbury's carefully plotted imagery juxtaposes binary opposites that represent the choices made by this society. This is exemplified by Montag's oxymoron, 'Kerosene ... is nothing but perfume to me' (p.13). The dichotomy also extends to certain characters. For example, Clarisse – whose name draws on the Latin root for 'brightness' – is identified with light, and therefore, by extrapolation, illumination or insight. Her skin is 'milk-white' (p.12) and she is dressed in white when Montag first meets her. This imagery presents a stark contrast to Montag, 'a minstrel man, burnt-corked' (p.10), and the unhappy darkness in which he lives. Whereas Clarisse's face emanates a soft light that reminds Montag of the 'rare and gently flattering light' (p.14) of a candle, his 'fiery' (p.10) smile is corrupted by the work he does, burnt into his face on a seemingly permanent basis.

Equally, the duality of fire itself is highlighted throughout the text. In the descriptions of the book burnings, the elegant images often belie the awfulness of the scene. For example, books are frequently described as birds: one of those belonging to the woman who sacrifices herself is 'a white pigeon, in [Montag's] hands, wings fluttering' (p.51). When Montag's own house burns, 'the books leapt and danced like roasted birds, their wings ablaze with red and yellow feathers' (p.151). However, the final image of the dead fire chief – 'twisted in on himself like a charred wax doll' (p.155) – leaves no doubt as to the unequivocal horror of fire's destructive power. With Montag's final understanding of its ability to warm and nourish, fire is likened to 'a winking eye' (p.187) that invites the fireman in from the shadows: 'He had never thought in his life that it could give as well as take. Even its smell was different' (p.187).

Intertextuality

Intertextuality is a key feature of *Fahrenheit 451*, with several other texts being referenced throughout. These allusions – usually quoted by the widely read Captain Beatty – link back to the central premise at the heart of the novel: the critical importance of literacy in a free society. Beatty's references, designed to bolster the argument for state-imposed censorship, ironically become a celebration of his own literacy, as well as providing an artful commentary on the interaction taking place.

One of the most telling references cited is 'Dover Beach', the lyric poem written by English poet Matthew Arnold in the nineteenth century. This poem, about the death of faith, has particular application to the society created by the powerbrokers in *Fahrenheit 451* – a world with 'neither joy, nor love, nor light' (p.130). Racked with fear and self-doubt, the characters in the novel no longer have faith in themselves. Arnold's message is so powerful that it even resonates with the foolish Mrs Phelps, though she is incapable of articulating why she is so distressed by Montag's reading.

Narrative point of view

Fahrenheit 451 is written in the third person, but exclusively from the point of view of the protagonist. This is established in the opening sentences, where the use of an unidentified 'he' immediately sets up a relationship with the character subsequently introduced as Montag. The intimate sharing of Montag's thoughts and feelings invites empathy from, and collusion with, the reader in much the same way as a first-person narration might. The limited perspective also raises some of the same questions about reliability and accuracy.

The narrative charts Montag's private struggle as he comes to terms with the oppressive system in which he has played an integral part. His voice shifts throughout the text, from complacent to confused, to angry, to humble. Montag is an unlikely hero. Nothing in his background as a fireman has prepared him for the personal journey on which he embarks. He is consistently indecisive and often overreactive. Nevertheless, he makes the '*right* kind of mistakes' (p.193), retaining readers' sympathy in spite – or perhaps because – of his flaws.

To what extent is the fireman a reliable narrator? Unlike his self-deceiving wife, Montag is honest; he is prepared to look squarely at his society and challenge its priorities. When Clarisse asks Montag about his own happiness, he mulls over the implications of her question – 'What does she think? I'm *not*?' (p.17) – trying to tease out the truth. Equally, he takes responsibility for his many errors of judgement – a rare quality in a society in which lack of responsibility is a defining characteristic.

However, Montag's understanding is hampered by his own ignorance and the new and unfamiliar territory into which he is venturing. As he grapples with the ideas presented to him by other characters – Clarisse, Beatty, Faber and Granger – his vulnerability is evident. The narrative voice captures these limitations of experience and understanding. For example, his lack of sophistication is evident in the exchanges with Beatty; he is easily outmanoeuvred by the wily fire chief. After killing Beatty, Montag's internal monologue reveals his confusion and remorse: 'you're a fool, a damn fool ... look at the mess and where's the mop?' (p.157).

By the end of the novel, the physical and emotional distance Montag has travelled is huge. He realises that the future needs to embrace a different way of seeing the world and, in particular, encompass an appreciation of the natural world. Having grown in confidence and insight, he is finally able to remember the biblical lines that have, thus far, eluded him.

Significance of the title

As the epigraph at the beginning of the novel notes, Fahrenheit 451 (about 233 degrees Celcius) is 'the temperature at which book-paper catches fire and burns'. Hence the title is an indirect reference to the book burning that becomes a metaphor for control. Books represent intellectual freedom, and the government has decreed that the ideas and information they contain pose a threat to social harmony. Firemen are now the 'official censors, judges, and executors' (p.77), charged with the destruction of the illicit material that could incite insurrection. From the arresting opening sentence – 'It was a pleasure to burn' (p.10) – fire is established as a central motif in the text.

CHAPTER-BY-CHAPTER ANALYSIS

PART ONE: The Hearth and the Salamander (pp.7–89)

Summary (pp.9–55): *Montag meets his new neighbour, Clarisse McClellan; his wife Mildred overdoses on sleeping pills; the Mechanical Hound threatens Montag; Clarisse disappears; a woman refuses to vacate her house when threatened by the firemen and burns to death.*

Firemen, such as the protagonist Guy Montag, play an integral role in Bradbury's re-imagined America, where democracy has morphed into totalitarianism and books are forbidden. Montag relishes his work. The accoutrements of his profession – the helmet numbered 451, the salamander insignia, the phoenix-disc and even the fire hose like a 'great python spitting its venomous kerosene upon the world' (p.9) – proclaim power and an elite privilege. Montag and his colleagues operate as one intimidating unit, machine-like in their commitment to serving the State. There is no room for independence or originality – in fact, they are 'all mirror-images' of Montag himself (p.46). Chosen for 'their looks as well as their proclivities' (p.46), every fireman has black hair and eyebrows, and a ruddy, ash-smeared complexion. As a group, they exemplify the notion that everyone 'must all be alike' (p.77).

Whereas the fireman and his wife embody the values of their society – he, by virtue of his position; she, by her wholesale consumption of what society has to offer – Clarisse and her family live differently. The McClellans eschew the empty pursuit of pleasure that keeps their peers entertained, choosing instead to spend their time interacting with one another. Montag remarks that Clarisse's face is 'like a mirror' (p.18), inviting him to consider his own sense of self in a way that staring in the firehouse mirror does not allow. The unexpectedly frank questions Clarisse asks Montag when they first meet and the ideas she invites him to consider thereafter are in direct contrast to Mildred's evasiveness.

Clarisse's observations, in fact, describe Montag's own experience: 'People don't talk about anything' (p.43). Montag's short-lived friendship with his young neighbour crystallises the dissatisfaction that has been brewing in him, and he realises that his happiness is an illusion.

Montag's marriage has been part of that illusion; in reality, the union is as cold and loveless as their bedroom. Entering this communal space, Montag is plunged into complete darkness, a soundless, airless, 'tomb-world' (p.19). His wife's overdose is a brutal wake-up call. Montag numbly observes that the machine hooked up to Mildred is another kind of snake, an invasive 'black cobra' (pp.22–3) with an Eye that 'sees' into her very soul, sucking out the poison, before fresh blood and serum are pumped back into her body. While she is physically revitalised by this process, Montag wishes that 'they could have taken her mind along to the dry-cleaner's' (p.25). Suicide attempts such as these are so routine in the community that they are not even attended by emergency MDs (paramedics). All that is needed are two 'handymen' (p.24) who clean up the problem briskly before moving on to the next case. The whole episode exposes a deeply embedded societal malaise.

Montag's personal troubles are played out against the backdrop of impending war. Overhead, the screaming jets foreshadow Mildred's actual death and the destruction of the city. Montag feels 'cut in half' by the pulverising sound, and imagines that in the morning the earth will be covered in dust 'like a strange snow' (p.22).

Naively, Montag starts to give himself away at work through the questions he asks. Foolishly, he even uses the iconic phrase 'Once upon a time' (p.47) after seeing it in a book of fairytales that he glanced at during a previous fire. Paradoxically, it is history that has now morphed into a fairytale: truth has virtually disappeared under the weight of lies and obfuscation, and a new past has been written to accommodate the current government model. According to the firemen's rule-book, the Firemen of America were established in 1790, and the first fireman was Benjamin Franklin (p.48). This is an especially malicious distortion of the facts, given that Franklin was an exponent of individual rights and philosophically opposed to authoritarianism.

Bradbury draws attention to Montag's hands at the beginning of the book. Wielding the fire hose, his hands are those of 'some amazing conductor playing all the symphonies of blazing and burning to bring down the tatters and charcoal ruins of history' (p.9). Yet these same hands betray him, seemingly acting of their own accord, when he steals books – an act that will end his career. Montag's professional facade, in fact, hides another self, a 'subconscious idiot that ran babbling at times, quite independent of will, habit, and conscience' (p.18). This 'other self' (p.18) responds with horror to the final case on which he is called out, where the self-immolation of a woman forces him to confront his own culpability.

Montag is surprised when Beatty not only recognises the woman's last words, but also puts them in context. The quotation she cites is significant because it speaks to their own time – irony that is unlikely to be lost on the fire chief. Hugh Latimer and Nicholas Ridley were English martyrs who were burnt alive for their religious beliefs during the Reformation of the Church in sixteenth-century England. Latimer's final words – 'We shall this day light such a candle, by God's grace, in England, as I trust shall never be put out' (p.54) – echo the proud opposition of the woman herself and highlight the dangers such 'fanatics' (p.53) present to the regime. Her use of a match to threaten the firemen demonstrates how effective even the smallest act of rebellion can be if it is mounted with conviction and supported by principle.

Montag only has time to read one stolen sentence – 'Time has fallen asleep in the afternoon sunshine' (p.51) – before the house goes up in flames. The line is from an essay, 'Dreamthorp', by the nineteenth-century Scottish poet Alexander Smith, and evokes a rural Eden, where life is so peaceful that even time falls asleep. This is clearly the antithesis of the frenetic society against which Montag is starting to revolt.

Key vocabulary

Benjamin Franklin: one of the founding fathers of the United States, and its first postmaster-general. Franklin helped draft the Declaration of Independence and also founded many civic organisations, including Philadelphia's first fire department.

Tower of Babel: in a biblical story from the Book of Genesis, humanity is punished by God for its hubris in building a tower designed to reach the heavens. As a result, people can no longer understand or speak a common language.

Q How does Bradbury establish the social and political context of his story?

Q What are your first impressions of these characters?

Q Why is Montag so afraid of the Mechanical Hound?

Summary (pp.55–89): *Montag steals another book; he refuses to go into work; Mildred confirms Clarisse's death; Beatty visits the fireman at home and gives a lecture; Montag argues with Mildred; the pair start to read.*

Mildred is so completely self-absorbed that she doesn't tell her husband about Clarisse's fatal accident or their neighbours' departure until four days after the event. Even then, Montag finds out by default. The girl's death is of little importance to his wife, as is the case of the woman who burned with her books. Mildred is incapable of empathising with her husband's distress, and is focused solely on the threat to her own lifestyle. Whether due to her over-reliance on medication or the intellectual slurry she absorbs day after day from the televisors, Mildred's memory is poor and her concentration weak. Like the parlour games, her verbal exchanges circle in a repetitive loop, unnervingly devoid of any actual substance.

Interestingly, professional reluctance within the firemen's ranks is not unusual and Beatty, familiar with the pattern, has suspected Montag of 'a guilty conscience' (p.39) for some time. When Montag fakes illness, Beatty believes this is just another case in which heavy-handed persuasion will allay misgivings. His lecture provides Montag – and the reader – with critical insight into why and how their society evolved, fleshing out the historical background that has led to the current vilification of books. The exponential population growth ran in tandem with an overwhelming number of alternative ways for people to fill their time. Books were condensed to such an extent that the content was reduced to headlines and sound bites, ultimately devoid of any academic capital. This 'intellectual pattern' has taken the people 'back to the nursery' (p.72). Finally, books became so discredited that an opportunistic government – seeing how cultural illiteracy might play into its hands – was able to exploit the trend.

Mildred, threatening to expose Montag's theft as she fusses with his pillow, personifies the very intellectual debasement that Beatty is talking about. As if to prove the point, when Mildred leaves the bedroom she reverts to watching the televisors and Beatty's lecture continues against the mind-numbing backdrop of the hysterical laughter coming from the parlour 'aunts' and 'uncles' (p.75). The government's objective is to have the minds of the public drink 'less and less' (p.75), thereby ensuring compliance. The fire chief's description of the cynical process designed to discourage the effects of reading – 'Whirl man's mind around about so fast under the pumping hands of publishers, exploiters, broadcasters, that the centrifuge flings off all unnecessary, time-wasting thought!' (p.73) – accurately reflects Montag's reaction to the parlour walls. Watching Mildred's program, he feels battered, as if he was 'a victim of concussion' (p.60).

Advising Montag to take the evening off, Beatty expects that his sermon will dampen the fireman's curiosity. However, instead of 'spinning happily' (p.76), Montag retains his desire to understand what the books have to offer. Despite his wife's objections, he retrieves his hidden contraband and starts to read.

By coincidence, Montag has chosen *Gulliver's Travels* by Jonathan Swift, an eighteenth-century political satire that criticises the corruption and arrogance of government. One line in particular – 'It is computed that eleven thousand persons have at several times suffered death rather than submit to break eggs at the smaller end' (p.89) – has direct application to Montag's own society. Some of the Lilliputians are willing to sacrifice themselves, rather than submit to the edict that requires everyone to eat from the same end of an egg. On the one hand, this deliberately absurd scenario highlights the dangers of blind conformity. On the other, separate to the triviality of the issue itself, it is also about refusing to yield to the tyranny of the majority and dying for one's principles.

Key point

Montag is at a crossroads. A number of factors converge to realign his thinking and lead him to an understanding of the corrupt nature of his society. By rejecting its values, Montag – like Gulliver – embarks on a journey into the unknown whose direction and outcome are both uncertain.

Q What does Beatty mean by 'Things began to have *mass*' (p.71)?

Q How does Mildred react to her husband's stance? Why does she finally acquiesce and start reading herself?

Q How does the quotation from *Gulliver's Travels* relate to the new America and to Montag's own situation?

The Sieve and the Sand (pp.91–143)

Summary (pp.93–120): *Montag and Mildred argue; Montag visits Professor Faber, who agrees to help him and gives him an audio-capsule.*

Montag feels defeated by his wife's attitude. Fearful and closed-minded, Mildred continues to insist that, contrary to all the evidence, she is happy; the worst possibility she can imagine is that Beatty might come and burn the house. The fire chief is too shrewd not to allow for error, and so sends the Mechanical Hound around again as a warning to Montag.

The Hound remains a sinister presence throughout the novel, an instrument of terror that symbolises the undisguised malevolence of the government. Montag anthropomorphises it, which adds to his fear. He does the same thing with the snake that purges his wife: 'It was dead but it was alive. It could see but it couldn't see' (p.95). As far as Montag is concerned, the existence of these human-like machines and the malign roles they play are symptomatic of the problem he is trying to solve. The subway train in which Montag travels is another kind of 'snake', hissing before it vanishes down its hole in the earth (p.104). For Montag, the journey is akin to being trapped in one of Mildred's intolerable parlour games. Commuters are 'pounded into submission' by the loud, rhythmic banalities that are 'vomited' over the train radio, advertising products such as 'Denham's Dentifrice' (p.103).

Painfully, Montag begins to understand the enormity of the task he is attempting. Knowledge is elusive and hard to grasp, like sand, and the difficulty of retaining it is analogous to sand pouring through a sieve. Montag is reminded of a childhood experience when he was at the beach, trying to fill a sieve with sand: the faster he poured, the faster the sand sifted through. Similarly, attempting to memorise the words contained in the stolen Bible, he feels overwhelmed by the 'terrible logic' (p.102) of his own ignorance.

It is an act of faith for Montag to seek Faber out. The fireman is desperate for someone to understand and share his concerns: 'But where do you get help, where do you find a teacher this late?' (p.97). At first, Faber resists offering his support. The old man is pessimistic about the future, believing that any who do survive the oncoming war are likely to start the process all over again. Significantly, he changes his mind when Montag starts to tear the book; in spite of himself, he cannot bear to see it destroyed. Montag is intuitively correct when he predicts events at the end of the text: 'There has to be someone ready when it [their civilisation] blows up' (p.114).

Throughout *Fahrenheit 451*, there is a pivotal debate between absolutism – as represented by Beatty – and freedom of thought – as represented by Professor Faber. These characters are figuratively pitched against each other, both proselytising for Montag's benefit, each laying out their cases and articulating the choices the fireman has to choose from. Faber cares so deeply about the state of their society that he feels 'sick' (p.114), and his 'revolutionary spirit' (p.117) has inspired him to create the audio-capsule as a small act of rebellion against the status quo. Unlike the Seashells, which are designed to shut down independent thought, promulgating propaganda and mindless entertainment in equal measure, Faber's device 'listens' (p.117). The little 'green bullet' (p.118) is interactive, inviting spontaneous discourse and uncensored opinion. For Montag, it is a pathway to a radical new way of thinking.

Key vocabulary

Praetorian Guard: a special unit of the Imperial Roman army that acted as elite bodyguards to the emperor.

Q What does the colour green symbolise in the context of the novel?

Q Explain the distinction Faber is trying to make when he says, 'I don't talk *things* … I talk the *meaning* of things' (p.98).

Summary (pp.120–43): *Mildred's friends visit; Beatty toys with Montag; the firemen are called out to the Montags' house.*

The arrival of Mrs Phelps and Mrs Bowles throws Montag's fresh awareness into sharp relief; the juxtaposition of Faber's voice in his head and the women's conversation is both jarring and discombobulating. Bradbury's constructions of femininity are necessarily informed by the social context of the 1950s. Hence, the dynamic he presents assumes the traditional social paradigm that middle-class women are the homemakers, and their husbands the breadwinners. However, the society depicted in *Fahrenheit 451* reduces women's function even further, taking a lifestyle that is already passive and presenting it as a mindless routine of frivolous self-indulgence. Docile and unquestioning, Mildred and her friends have allowed themselves to be seduced, then manipulated, by whatever virtual trivia is on offer. In this sense, they are utterly complicit in their own intellectual and spiritual corruption.

The text explores the interplay between stasis and action. In spite of the loud, frenetic nature of American society, there is a peculiarly static quality about people's lives. Mildred and her friends are stuck on an elaborate treadmill that keeps them in continuous motion, but prevents them from doing anything of real value. In this sense, it is analogous to running on the spot. Their lives consist of visiting each other's houses on rotation to watch the same strident, inane programs they could watch at home. Listening to the women, Montag feels disconnected and alienated, as if he is in a foreign store where his currency is 'strange and unusable' (p.124). Privately, he considers the women to be 'monsters' (p.127), and blames them for their vacuous pursuit of pleasure at the expense of meaningful relationships. However, his attempt to jolt them out of their complacency by reading to them simply reinforces the divide between them all.

'Dover Beach' by Matthew Arnold sums up Montag's painful, nascent awareness of the state of his society: 'And we are here as on a darkling plain / Swept with confused alarms of struggle and flight' (p.130). He can feel himself turning into a hybrid man – 'Montag-plus-Faber, fire plus water' (p.133) – and trusts that, eventually, he can be wiser about the things that matter. Bradbury references the New Testament story of Cana, where Christ performed his first public miracle, turning water into wine at a wedding feast. Similarly, Montag believes that, with the old professor's help, 'after everything had mixed and simmered and worked away in silence, there would be neither fire nor water, but wine' (p.133).

With Beatty, however, Montag finds himself completely out of his depth. The fire chief draws on his formidable literary knowledge to taunt and confuse Montag, rebutting arguments that the latter cannot even articulate. Beatty takes a perverse delight in undermining Montag's newfound intellectual curiosity, emphasising the inherently 'treacherous' nature of books: 'You think they're backing you up, and they turn on you' (p.139).

In retrospect, Montag should have been more alert to the danger he was in. The Hound had been sent to his house on at least two occasions, and his reckless loss of control in front of Mildred and her friends simply incriminates him in their unsympathetic eyes, thereby inviting reprisal. After his anger abates and regret sets in, he can see them as 'chaff women ... with the kernels blown out from under them by a neon wind' (p.141), incapable of change. Despite knowing that he has been a fool, Montag is still shocked when the fire truck pulls up outside his house. Like the Hound, the Salamander is another menacing representation of the power of the State, personified as a 'gaseous dragon' (p.141) that sleeps 'with its kerosene in its belly and the firethrowers crossed upon its flanks' (p.135).

Key point

Montag has shifted rapidly from a man to whom kerosene is 'perfume' (p.13) to one who 'vomit[s]' (p.66) at the smell. However, his journey towards wisdom is polarising, with lasting consequences for his marriage, career and liberty.

Q What does Faber mean when he says of Captain Beatty, 'He could be one of us' (p.118)?

Q Discuss the following quotations and how they relate to the themes of *Fahrenheit 451*.

- 'A little learning is a dangerous thing.' (p.137)
- 'Knowledge is more than equivalent to force.' (p.138)
- 'Knowledge is power!' (p.138)

Burning Bright (pp.145–211)

Summary (pp.147–68): *Beatty directs Montag to burn his own house; Montag murders the fire chief; war is declared; Montag flees through the city; he plants books in a fireman's house.*

Mildred is inconsolable at the loss of her parlour relatives: 'Poor family, poor family, oh everything gone, everything, everything gone now' (p.148). Ignoring her husband, she is a pathetic, distracted figure as she flees the house. Without the lipstick that has helped define her face, her own mouth is also 'gone' (p.148).

Montag derives a perverse satisfaction from torching his own house. It seems fitting that this residence where he lived with 'a strange woman who would forget him tomorrow' (p.151) be consigned to the flames. When he gets to the parlour with its blank dormant walls, he cuts off 'its terrible emptiness' with 'a gift of one huge bright yellow flower of burning' (p.152). The burning attracts the usual voyeuristic crowd. In this society, where personal property can be destroyed with the flick of a flamethrower, ownership is ephemeral. Described as a 'carnival' (p.147) and a 'circus' (p.152), these burnings demonstrate the contempt in which individual rights are held and are a powerful way for the State to send its message regarding civic disobedience.

The final confrontation with Beatty leaves Montag in shock and fleeing for his life. Ironically, the fire chief foreshadows his own death. He hypothesises that fire is so attractive because it's 'the thing man wanted to invent but never did' (p.149), arguing that fire's real beauty lies in its capacity for destruction. However, one of the mistakes made by ideologues such as Beatty is the assumption that all problems – including 'responsibility and consequences' (p.150) – can be solved by incinerating them. He fails to realise that abstractions, such as intellectual freedom or moral resistance, cannot be dispensed with so easily.

Beatty's musings come to chilling fruition when Montag turns the flamethrower on him. Again, Montag's hands, representing his defiant self, act independently, continuing to exercise their own choices to flout the law. Beatty's demise, graphically described, is a terrifying illustration of the destructive power of fire: 'And then he was a shrieking blaze, a jumping, sprawling, gibbering mannikin, no longer human or known, all writhing flame on the lawn' (p.154). Afterwards, Montag mourns his loss of innocence, but decides that Beatty wanted to die. Whether this is fact or a comforting rationalisation, there is no doubt that the chief invites retribution from his panicked employee. In any case, Montag's choices are few: 'burn them or they'll burn you' (p.160).

Montag's desperate flight through the city illustrates just how perilous a place the urban environment can be, especially for a pedestrian. In terms of danger, there is little difference between the war that has now become a reality and the arbitrary violence that turns the streets into a war zone. The deadly exuberance of teenagers on the rampage, and their cavalier disregard for human life, is a frightening example of the amorality that characterises this society.

Q Why does Beatty ignore the first alarm put in by Mildred's friends?

Q Just before he turns the flamethrower on the fire chief, Montag says, 'We never burned *right* …' (p.154). Discuss the implications of this statement.

Q Why might Beatty have wanted to die?

Summary (pp.168–211): *Montag farewells Faber and escapes to the country; he meets up with Granger and his band of fellow academics; an atomic bomb destroys the city.*

For Montag, Faber is the one secure anchor point in a world that has spun rapidly out of control. The speed with which events have turned the fireman's life around in a few short days leaves him bewildered. Yet Montag also knows that his previous life was a sham, and that he has been subconsciously moving towards this point for a long time: 'It saved itself up to happen … I went around doing one thing and feeling another' (p.169).

Reality television takes on new significance with the manhunt, which is watched on a million parlour walls. Montag is able to observe the Mechanical Hound through the windows he passes, reminding himself that this was 'no fictional episode … it was in actuality his own chess-game he was witnessing, move by move' (p.177). The authorities are ingenious in the way they enlist the collusion of the general public to catch Montag, exhorting everyone to look out of their doors and windows to identify the lone fugitive running through the streets. When their true objective is frustrated, an anonymous scapegoat is captured in a blaze of imagery that evokes the totalitarian nature of the regime: 'The helicopter light shot down a dozen brilliant pillars that built a cage all about the man' (p.191).

Floating down the river, Montag feels strangely calm: 'He was moving from an un-reality that was frightening into a reality that was unreal because it was new' (p.180). He finally has the time to reflect on the unsustainability of his old life. He realises that his society has been locked in an indefensible cycle that will ultimately result in existential destruction. When Montag finds the railroad track, he unhesitatingly recognises it as 'the path to wherever he was going' (p.186), the truth he is trying to discover. It is a leap of faith – 'he was surprised to learn how certain he suddenly was of a single fact he could not prove' (p.186) – but he understands it to be a journey that Clarisse herself undertook.

Granger and his group invite Montag to view the world from a different perspective. For the first time, he realises that fire can warm, as well as burn, and give as well as take. Montag is also struck by the silence of the countryside, which provides a profound change from the noise that has defined his life in the city. Indeed, the fireman wonders how his wife would cope with the silence. This contrast between noise and silence is woven through the text. For example, after his earlier confrontation with Mildred's friends, Montag berates himself, belatedly realising that he must think before acting: 'When would he stop being entirely mad and be quiet, be very quiet indeed?' (p.142). Silence is presented as a gift, the necessary antidote to the carefully orchestrated discord that is fed to the masses. Silence affords Granger's band the milieu in which to remember the precious cargo they carry in their heads.

Granger stresses to Montag that, as individuals, they are not important. Separately, all they had was impotent 'rage' (p.193); collectively they can make a difference. These men have a sacred mission, though, counterintuitively, it involves burning books. The true value of books lies in the ideas that they contain, ideas that can never be destroyed so long as there are people who care enough to remember them.

The assumption that a 'quick war' (p.122) is necessarily a good war is shown to be a bitter fallacy. The war – when it does come – is so blindingly fast that the bombs complete their deadly mission in seconds, reducing the city to 'baking-powder' (p.208) in an apocalyptic heartbeat. Montag speculates sadly on his wife's demise, wondering if she experienced any belated insight into the emptiness of her life. He imagines Mildred's final seconds of revelation: her darkened parlour walls become a mirror that reflects 'such a wildly empty face, all by itself in the room, touching nothing, starved and eating of itself, that at last she recognized it as her own' (p.204). Afterwards, Montag starts to remember the elusive verses from the Books of Ecclesiastes and Revelation that, up until now, he has struggled to retain. He trusts that this knowledge will be ultimately absorbed 'in the blood', which is the essence of every individual: 'I've got one finger on it now; that's a beginning' (p.207).

Traditionally, fire is seen as a cleansing agent that purges corruption and disease, a symbol of rebirth. Now that American cities have been burnt to the ground, there is an opportunity for society to redeem itself by rising from the ashes with different values and a fresh moral perspective. Bradbury's faith in human nature is expressed through Granger, who references the historical ability of people to reinvent themselves: 'But that's the wonderful thing about man; he never gets so discouraged or disgusted that he gives up doing it all over again, because he knows very well it is important and worth the doing' (p.197). The potent image of the Phoenix – 'first cousin to Man' (pp.208–9) – emerging from the ashes symbolises humanity's capacity to resurrect itself, as well as destroy itself.

As the men head towards the devastated city to help the survivors, Montag thinks again of the lines from Revelation: 'And on either side of the river was there a tree of life … And the leaves of the tree were for the healing of the nations' (p.211). These words celebrate the cycle of life, encapsulating the men's hopes for a better future. Nevertheless, the conclusion of the novel is cautionary, as well as optimistic. While Bradbury demonstrates faith in people's capacity to change, he also urges some critical soul-searching: 'Come on now, we're going to go build a mirror-factory first and put out nothing but mirrors for the next year and take a long look in them' (pp.209–10).

Key point

As well as being a symbol of humanity's resurrection, the Phoenix also represents Montag himself. As a fireman, he wore a phoenix-disc on the front of his uniform. By the end of the novel, he has risen from ignorance and darkness to a spiritual rebirth.

Key vocabulary

Keystone Cops: a series of silent black-and-white crime-comedy films made between 1912 and 1917.

Q What does Montag mean when he concludes that 'the guild of the asbestos-weaver must open shop very soon' (p.181)?

Q Granger comments, 'You haven't seen yourself in a mirror lately' (p.197). What do mirrors represent in the text?

Q Discuss these lines from Ecclesiastes: 'To everything there is a season. Yes. A time to break down, and a time to build up' (pp.210–11). How does this apply to *Fahrenheit 451*?

Q Do you think that human beings are clever enough to recognise, and ultimately avoid, the mistakes that lead to their destruction?

CHARACTERS & RELATIONSHIPS

Guy Montag

Key quotes

'I don't want to change sides and just be told what to do. There's no reason to change if I do that.' (p.120)

'At least you were a fool about the right things.' (Faber, p.168)

'"Don't judge a book by its cover," someone said.' (p.198)

Montag is a simple man who, on the face of it, has unquestioningly accepted the logic of his role in society. Like his father and grandfather before him, he is an instrument of repression, integral to the maintenance and preservation of the status quo, inciting awe and fear in equal measure. Montag relishes his profession, deriving genuine satisfaction from consigning forbidden material to the flames: 'It was a special pleasure to see things eaten, to see things blackened and changed' (p.9). He knows nothing of the history of book burning and, to date, has simply believed the fiction that it has been state-sanctioned since the eighteenth century.

In this sense, Montag is a reluctant revolutionary. He is defensive when Clarisse asks if he's happy – 'Of course I'm happy' (p.17) – but, on reflection, is forced to concede that his life, including his marriage, is profoundly unfulfilling. The initial conversation with Clarisse is immediately followed by the discovery of his wife's suicide attempt, an event that brings home to him the emptiness of their life together. The bedroom they share is like a 'cold marbled room of a mausoleum after the moon had set' (p.19).

From the outset, Clarisse recognises something different in Montag: 'You're not like the others' (p.34). Their friendship is unexpected and brief, but the guileless honesty of the girl makes a considerable, if occasionally unsettling, impression on Montag. Clarisse homes in on

Montag's willingness to listen and engage, qualities that are rare and especially at odds with his job as a fireman. In demanding honesty from him, Clarisse challenges Montag on a number of fronts. Walking with her becomes part of Montag's routine and he finds himself strangely comforted by her proximity.

In a similar way, Montag is drawn to Faber, and his random meeting with the old professor in the park sets him on a direct collision course with the government. With hindsight, Montag agrees with Faber that his resistance had been brewing for a long time: 'I went around doing one thing and feeling another' (p.169). The fact that Montag has been stealing books and hiding them in his home shows an impulsive curiosity that even he does not fully understand. In doing so, he jeopardises both his livelihood and his liberty. Yet he has flouted the law more than once and the presence of the cache hidden behind the grille remains a secret, guilty temptation.

The martyrdom of the old woman who chooses to burn with her books rather than face imprisonment is a turning point for Montag. Her courageous stand moves him profoundly. Coupled with the news of Clarisse's death, Montag's distress is such that he struggles to get out of bed. His boss, Beatty, underestimates Montag, initially regarding him as just another fireman with 'an itch' (p.81). He believes that he can manage Montag but, ironically, his lecture has the opposite effect, giving Montag a context and a background that further fuels his discontent. Literally having Faber's voice in his head invites Montag to rethink everything he has previously taken for granted: 'he could feel the start of the long journey, the leave-taking, the going away from the self he had been' (p.133).

Montag is a flawed hero who acts impetuously, propelled by instinct and a yearning for the truth. Faber calls him 'brave' (p.105), but the fireman does not always consider the consequences of his actions. Beatty compares him to Icarus – 'Old Montag wanted to fly near the sun and now that he's burnt his damn wings, he wonders why' (p.147) – and in a way, he is right. Montag *has* been impatient and ambitious, responding recklessly once he realises the way in which people are collaborating in their own oppression. Losing his temper with Mildred's friends achieves nothing except to vent his own frustrations. Worse, he alienates his wife completely and exposes himself as a dissident. Forced into a corner, Montag subsequently murders Beatty with confounding ease. Afterwards, he berates himself for his arrogance: 'Pride, damn it, and temper, and you've junked it all, at the very start you vomit on everyone and on yourself' (p.157).

By the time Montag has eluded the manhunt, and is out in the country, he becomes calmer. The more distance he places between himself and the city, the more peaceful and, indeed, vindicated he feels: 'He felt as if he had left a stage behind and many actors' (p.180). He becomes one of a handful of survivors who will be instrumental in safeguarding the knowledge that might shape a more hopeful future. Humbly, Montag prepares to play his part.

Key point

Montag is a man in search of his true self. His metamorphosis, from loyal servant of the State to committed rebel, provides the narrative arc of the story. His battle has been that of the underdog, fighting against overwhelming odds, but symbolically he takes the lead as Granger's band heads back towards the city.

Mildred Montag

Key quotes

'And suddenly she was so strange he couldn't believe he knew her at all.' (p.57)

'How long is it since you were really bothered? About something important, about something real?' (Montag, p.69)

'My wife's dying.' (Montag, p.105)

Mildred is a superficial, deeply disturbed woman, 'as thin as a praying mantis from dieting', with hair that has been 'burnt by chemicals to a brittle straw' (p.65). Everything about her appearance – from the 'reddened pouting lips' to the skin 'like white bacon' (p.65) – suggests artifice. Mildred has become increasingly disconnected from the actual world around her, including her husband. The couple sleep in separate beds – she 'never wanted any children' (p.40) – and neither physical intimacy nor meaningful conversation intrude on the bland monotony of their relationship.

When the pair do share the same space, Mildred closes herself off, seduced by the simulated reality presented by the Seashells. She has the little thimble radios plugged into her ears on a semi-permanent basis, even when she is supposedly sleeping: 'There had been no night in the last two years that Mildred had not swum in that sea' (p.20). Like the Seashells, her parlour walls are an addiction, designed to beguile and desensitise. Mildred does not consider the three existing screens sufficient and, despite the prohibitive cost, tries to persuade her husband to buy another for the remaining fourth wall. Mildred's day seems to revolve around the steady diet of interactive programming delivered by the screens. She is heavily invested in the array of characters that have become her 'real' family but, when asked what the latest script is actually about, can only repeat, 'It's really fun' (p.30).

On face value, Mildred is shallow and frivolous. Yet there are flashes of intuition – 'Hey … The man's *thinking*!' (p.29) – that might suggest this was not always the case. Montag holds onto the increasingly faint hope that there is a version of his wife, 'another Mildred', who is buried 'so deep inside this one, and so bothered, really bothered, that the two women had never met' (p.69). Beneath the sanguine image, Mildred is so unhappy that she anesthetises herself with pills and has attempted suicide on more than one occasion. However, she stubbornly refuses to acknowledge – let alone discuss – her latest attempt, telling Montag, 'Never in a billion years' (p.29). This capacity for self-denial is what allows Mildred to function in the treacherous world in which she finds herself. Immersion in the noise and colour of the parlour games drowns out disquiet or doubt. At the same time, she does admit to feeling angry, and habitually drives through the night at high speed as a way of venting her frustrations: 'It's fun out in the country. You hit rabbits, sometimes you hit dogs' (p.84).

Mildred is fiercely protective of her comfortable lifestyle and too much of a coward to jeopardise it. Self-preservation remains her primary agenda. Predictably, she refuses to become a co-conspirator in Montag's quest for knowledge. Mildred is frightened by her husband's determination to flout the rules, and she distances herself from his growing obsession with books. Finally, in an act of craven disloyalty, she betrays her husband by denouncing him to the authorities.

Key point

Mildred is both an offender and a victim. She exemplifies the compliant – and complacent – majority, having accepted the prevailing social narrative and its empty fiction of what constitutes 'happiness'. However, this does not save her, and she becomes one of the casualties of America's folly.

Clarisse McClellan

Key quotes

'I'm seventeen and I'm crazy.' (p.14)

'I like to smell things and look at things, and sometimes stay up all night, walking, and watch the sun rise.' (p.14)

'She was a time bomb ... She didn't want to know how a thing was done, but why.' (Beatty, p.79)

Clarisse is the antithesis of Mildred: intuitive, independent, intellectually curious and fearless in her determination to explore the world. She comes from a '*most* peculiar' (p.17) family, whose members spend their evenings simply talking – something that Montag finds baffling. Her uncle has been a particular influence on her and she has absorbed many of his ideas. Unlike her peers, Clarisse rarely watches the parlour walls or goes to the fun parks. She avoids school when she can, dismissing it as a frustrating exercise in rote learning where students are force-fed information rather than encouraged to think for themselves. Instead, she prefers to walk in the rain, observe people and reflect on what is going on around her. Although Clarisse sees a psychiatrist regularly for the sake of appearances – 'They *make* me go' (p.33) – in general, she is left to her own devices.

Montag feels Clarisse's presence before he actually meets her: 'The air seemed charged with a special calm as if someone had waited there' (p.11). Stopping to walk back with him, she proceeds to engage him in conversation, undeterred by his age or his status as a fireman. Montag is intrigued by her face, which seems to reveal something of himself, reflecting his 'innermost trembling thought' (p.18). In the absence of books, Clarisse asks questions. Even though Montag tells her uneasily that she thinks 'too many things' (p.16), he finds her candour hard to resist, even when she hits a personal nerve: 'You're peculiar, you're aggravating, yet you're easy to forgive' (p.34). For Clarisse, the world is an exciting place and no topic of conversation is unworthy, or off limits. In her talks with Montag, she switches subjects constantly, challenging his complacency, and causing him to reconsider aspects of his own life. More than once, he is struck by her maturity. According to her therapist, she is 'a regular onion' because she keeps him busy 'peeling away the layers' (p.33).

Clarisse foreshadows her own shocking death when she tells Montag that ten of her friends were killed in car accidents in the past year alone. Beatty dismisses the tragedy, revealing that the family had been under surveillance, and even suggesting the fatality was to the government's advantage. The fire chief regards people like the McClellans as dangerous; Clarisse was 'one of those damn do-gooders with their shocked, holier-than-thou silences, their one talent making others feel guilty' (p.148). For Montag though, her legacy is a positive one. He is reminded of his young neighbour when he finds the railroad track, 'the magic charm' (p.186) that will lead him to the future. For no reason he can prove, he is convinced that, at some point, Clarisse walked on the same path, alert to the beauty of the countryside and buoyed by her own brand of infectious optimism.

Captain Beatty

Key quotes

'His voice is like butter.' (Montag, p.116)

'But remember that the Captain belongs to the most dangerous enemy of truth and freedom …' (Faber, p.140)

'Go ahead now, you second-hand litterateur, pull the trigger.' (p.154)

Captain Beatty is a dangerous adversary, an experienced, cynical misanthrope who masks his fanatical devotion to his calling under a veneer of affability. He is exceptionally well read, throwing around quotations at will, and utterly disarming the ignorant Montag, who is no match for his shrewd superior.

Although Beatty strongly suspects that Montag has been stealing forbidden material, he is initially inclined to give his employee the benefit of the doubt. Alerted by Montag uttering the fatal phrase, 'I've been thinking' (p.46), Beatty is surprisingly tolerant, taking it upon himself to 'educate' the fireman and deliver a lecture on the history of their profession. Moreover, the chief does not act immediately when Mildred's friends call in the alarm on Montag, but waits until Mildred herself informs on her husband. Beatty understands the seductive power of books, effectively admitting to Montag that he, too, has been tempted by the learning they contain: 'Read a few lines and off you go over the cliff … I know, I've been through it all' (p.137). Nevertheless, Beatty's monologue at the station shows how 'slippery' (p.138) he can be in the service of the status quo. Sardonically, he tells Montag, 'I was doing a terrible thing in using the very books you clung to, to rebut you on every hand, on every point!' (p.139).

Beatty is a poker player. Beneath the genial facade is a ruthless, deeply embittered man who has nothing but contempt for his fellow human beings. The anger that is usually controlled rises to the surface in his final confrontation with Montag. Beatty is brutally sarcastic, mocking the fireman's friendship with Clarisse: 'Look at the sick look on your face' (p.148). His real vitriol, though, is reserved for Clarisse herself, and her kind, whom he blames for any discontent that may spread in the community: 'God damn, they rise like the midnight sun to sweat you in your bed!' (p.148). In retrospect, Montag concludes that Beatty wanted to die. Certainly, the fire chief does everything to provoke the situation, continuing to goad Montag even when the latter threatens him with a flamethrower.

Given that Beatty is clearly clever and well read, Bradbury's comments (in his introduction to the 50th Anniversary Edition, p.5) as to why the fire chief became 'a burner of books' are interesting. Beatty had 'once been a wanderer of libraries and a lover of the finest literature in history', but had become disillusioned when books could not provide the help he needed after adversity struck: 'Turning on them, he lit a match' (p.5). Beatty's career is based on the arrogant assumption that fire can always be controlled for his own purposes. However, this is dispelled by his terrible death, which highlights how, just as easily, fire can become a weapon.

Key point

Beatty's ability to use the knowledge he has gleaned from books in order to justify the purge against them is as effective as it is ironic.

Professor Faber

Key quotes

'Mr Montag, you are looking at a coward. I saw the way things were going, a long time back. I said nothing.' (p.106)

'I care so much I'm sick.' (p.114)

Just as Clarisse represents a complete contrast to Mildred, Faber is set in opposition to Captain Beatty, presenting the counterargument to the fire chief's rhetoric. Like Beatty, Faber is an educated man of letters, whose memory and experience predates the current purge. As a retired English professor who lost his university position many years earlier, Faber is a casualty of the new order. Elderly, alone and painfully aware of his limitations, Faber leads a timid existence, rarely venturing outside his house. Until he meets Montag, the professor has kept as low a profile as possible. At first, therefore, he resists the fireman's newly kindled zeal to affect change; he only agrees to work with Montag when the latter threatens to destroy the stolen Bible.

However, Faber is more courageous than he gives himself credit for. He takes a considerable risk in quoting poetry to Montag at their first meeting and voluntarily giving out his address. He also exposes himself when he trusts Montag with his ingenious little audio-capsule – a death sentence if it were traced back to him, given its subversive intent. Though Faber defines himself as an apathetic coward and feels ongoing remorse for his failure to act when he had the opportunity, he still yearns to do something. He tells Montag, 'I've waited, trembling, half a lifetime for someone to speak to me' (p.117). Faber corroborates Beatty's argument that the public itself stopped reading 'of its own accord' (p.113). Like the fire chief, Faber has become cynical about people's capacity or willingness to change, but, unlike the chief, he retains some hope for the future.

Faber proves himself a worthy ally. After Beatty's death, rather than being cowed by Montag's recklessness, the old man seems energised: 'I feel alive for the first time in years' (p.169). He does not blame Montag for placing him in danger, instead offering moral support as well as invaluable practical advice. Faber is saved by his own decision to leave the city and, determined to make amends for his former passivity, the professor plans his next step with a renewed sense of purpose: 'I feel I'm doing what I should have done a lifetime ago' (p.169).

Granger

Key quotes

'We all made the *right* kind of mistakes, or we wouldn't be here.' (p.193)

'When the war's over, perhaps we can be of some use in the world.' (p.196)

Granger is the unofficial leader of a little band of 'old Harvard degrees' (p.170) who have survived by getting out of the cities and moving around the countryside. By virtue of their academic backgrounds, these men are considered subversives, but the government has declined to waste resources hunting them down. Granger himself became a fugitive when he struck a fireman who came to burn his library.

Granger and his friends are part of a wider network who act as the custodians of memory – literally 'bums on the outside, libraries inside' (p.196). Their strategy is simple, but ingenious. They cannot rely on books – indeed, they too are 'book-burners' (p.194). Instead, every man stores critical information safely in his head, 'where no one can see it or suspect it' (p.195). While the 'bits and pieces' (p.195) memorised by each individual are just a tiny part of a vast whole, collectively the group represents a powerful body of retained scholarship. This responsibility informs their behaviour. Mindful of the danger, Granger insists, 'We're not out to incite or anger anyone yet. For if we are destroyed, the knowledge is dead, perhaps for good' (p.195).

Granger has been significantly influenced by his grandfather, a man whose contribution to the world Granger clearly admires. He encouraged his grandson to ask questions, reject complacency and live life to the fullest. Granger is optimistic about the future. Fired by a sense of mission, he argues that, with time, there will be more and more people who remember and learn from the past: 'That's where we'll win out in the long run' (p.209). The implied caveat is that people need to be perceptive enough to listen.

Mrs Bowles and Mrs Phelps

Key quote

'Did you hear them, did you hear these monsters talking about monsters?' (Montag, p.127)

Mildred's friends are a vacuous pair, as obsessed with appearances and the selfish pursuit of pleasure as Mildred herself. Their preferred topic of conversation is the latest show on the televisors and they react with 'unconcealed irritation' (p.122) when Montag switches off the parlour walls, suggesting that they talk instead. Even the forthcoming war fails to touch them. Their husbands have been recruited in its service, but neither the deadly nature of war nor their spouses' welfare is of concern to them. Mrs Phelps' airy confidence that 'it's always someone else's husband [who] dies' (p.123) – usually by suicide – reveals a casual indifference that belies the imminent danger confronting them all.

Mrs Phelps is childless – 'No one in his right mind ... would have children!' (p.124) – while Mrs Bowles' idea of parenting is to have as little to do with her children as possible. They are put in school most of the time and the televisors take care of the rest: 'You heave them into the "parlour" and turn the switch' (p.125). These women studiously avoid anything to do with genuine emotion and, though Clara Phelps is at least capable of responding to Montag's reading of 'Dover Beach', she is unable to articulate the source of her distress. The two women are alarmed and angered by Montag's erratic behaviour and, undeterred by their so-called friendship with Mildred, call in the alarm on the fireman at the earliest opportunity.

THEMES, IDEAS & VALUES

Authority and control

Key quotes

'Any man's insane who thinks he can fool the Government and us.' (Beatty, p.46)

'It didn't come from the Government down ... Technology, mass exploitation, and minority pressure carried the trick, thank God.' (Beatty, p.76)

In the future envisaged by Bradbury, the United States has become a totalitarian state, authoritarian in its domestic policy and aggressive internationally. We are told that the country has 'started and won two atomic wars since 1960' (p.96). The imminent prospect of retaliation is ever-present, yet the threat of war seems of little concern to most citizens. The bombers that regularly cross the sky are studiously ignored by the average citizen and political commentators alike. While the US is more prosperous than ever before, its reputation as a principled global player has vanished; the nation is now 'hated' (p.96) and feared, rather than admired. Its insularity and isolationist stance have made it utterly indifferent to the distress and poverty suffered by other countries: 'I've heard rumours; the world is starving, but we're well-fed ... the world works hard and we play' (p.96).

The governing regime works from the premise that its citizens' compliance will be ensured if controversy is eliminated: 'If you don't want a man unhappy politically, don't give him two sides to a question to worry him; give him one. Better yet, give him none' (p.80). Books present an obvious threat to the omnipresent complacency, so firemen have been given a new job as 'custodians of our peace of mind' (p.77). Anyone found with books in their possession is arrested and incarcerated, and their house is burned to the ground. Beatty cynically calls his men 'the Happiness Boys' (p.81), telling Montag that they stand against 'the small tide of those who want to make everyone unhappy with conflicting theory and thought' (p.81). If everybody thinks alike – or, better still, doesn't think at all – then the likelihood of conflict is essentially eradicated.

Like the rulers of ancient Rome, the government uses 'bread and circuses' to keep its citizens well fed and entertained, thus minimising the risk of civil disobedience. Even the implementation of the law has been turned into a communal spectacle that has its own entertainment value. Montag realises that the firemen are always called out at night: 'Is it because the fire is prettier by night? More spectacle, a better show?' (p.53). When his own house burns, it attracts the usual crowd who are happy to watch smugly from the sidelines. The burnings also evoke the public executions of past centuries. They act primarily as a visceral warning; the dread they incite is a powerful deterrent and another way of ensuring the complicity of the general population.

Nothing is allowed to get in the way of the authorities' single-minded pursuit of their agenda. Even after war is declared, 'the circus must go on' (p.172). The manhunt for Montag is turned into live theatre, beamed into millions of parlour walls to provide a vicarious thrill for the audience watching and demonstrate the efficiency of the law. Variously described as a 'big game', a 'hunt' and a 'one-man carnival' (p.173), the show only comes to its 'snap ending' (p.190) when the Mechanical Hound pounces on its nameless victim. As it happens, the latter's identity or innocence is irrelevant. Saving face is critical and, for the benefit of the viewers, the police require an immediate scapegoat 'to end things with a bang' (p.190).

Prosperity and the veneer of contentment mask the terror under which most civilians live. The populace is expected to conform; dissent is supressed ruthlessly. Montag's case highlights the lack of judicial procedure, which includes the presumption of innocence until proven guilty; dissidents can be imprisoned without trial or murdered in the street. The most trivial behaviour becomes illicit if it deviates from the norm. Clarisse's uncle has been jailed for two days for driving too slowly on a freeway. He was also arrested for simply being a pedestrian as walking along the street has become a rare – possibly criminal – activity. The US is a nation of spies and eavesdroppers; people are expected to inform on their friends and neighbours as part of their civic duty. The government is alert to every initiative – however hypothetical – that may compromise the social contract. Having a lengthy conversation is now considered a potentially subversive activity. Bizarrely, houses no longer feature front porches as they encouraged people to sit and interact at leisure. From the government's perspective, this is 'the wrong *kind* of social life' (p.83), and not in keeping with its preference to keep people constantly on the move.

These restrictions have become the norm and few people think to question them. However, as Beatty explains, 'You can't rid yourselves of all the odd ducks in just a few years' (p.79). People such as the McClellans, who have a suspicious history, are monitored closely and dossiers are kept on each member of the family. Recognising the critical influence of the home environment, the government has tried to minimise the amount of time children spend there. Hence, the kindergarten age has been lowered year after year until 'now we're almost snatching them from the cradle' (p.79). Once in school, children are a captive audience. Like every other aspect of this society, the education system is tightly controlled. Clarisse's description of school makes it appear similar to an indoctrination camp, where the students are fed misinformation and propaganda from a screen, and discouraged from asking questions or thinking independently. She is clever enough to realise that 'it's a lot of funnels and a lot of water poured down the spout and out the bottom, and them telling us it's wine when it's not' (p.42).

Censorship and lost knowledge

Key quotes

'... the word "intellectual", of course, became the swear word it deserved to be.' (Beatty, p.76)

'The books are to remind us what asses and fools we are. They're Caesar's praetorian guard, whispering as the parade roars down the avenue, "Remember, Caesar, thou art mortal".' (Faber, p.112)

Montag finds himself in a world in which intellectual enquiry has become the enemy. Beatty complains that 'none of these books agree with each other' (p.52), as if to suggest that truth is an absolute and there is only one truth for everyone. He is, of course, being disingenuous, as he knows, better than most, that diversity of thought is essential to independent and rigorous scholarship. This points to the fundamental paradox underpinning the vilification of books. On the one hand, they are disparaged as contradictory and, therefore, inconsequential. On the other, they are clearly regarded as dangerous, a pernicious influence that will corrupt a compliant population.

Books are the symbol of intellectual worth, the key repository of knowledge that has been lost. Faber explains to Montag that it is not the books themselves that are 'magical' (p.108). The magic is in what books 'say' (p.108), the way in which they try to make sense of the world and people's place in it by presenting ideas of quality and substance. These ideas stimulate debate. The novel argues that once individuals stop actively seeking knowledge through books, then they stop asking questions; they become passive and easily manipulated. Further, Faber maintains that individuals – having been denied high-quality information and the leisure to digest it – have been robbed of the opportunity to act on what they might have learned.

Books are hated and feared by the authorities because they show 'the pores in the face of life' (p.108). By contrast, the culture does everything to eradicate those pores, representing life in as sanitised a way as possible. *Fahrenheit 451* anticipates the concept of political correctness, an idea that did not gain traction until the mid-1970s. Beatty argues that 'the bigger your market ... the less you handle controversy' (pp.75–6). Placating the sensibilities of the many minority groups has become a driving imperative. This has direct implications for writers and other creative thinkers who, in the past, have been the ones articulating challenging ideas. Now, content is safely, universally bland, 'a nice blend of vanilla tapioca' (p.76).

Disturbingly, people have been complicit in their own repression. Beatty is at pains to point out to Montag that the current constraints were not initiated by the government: 'There was no dictum, no declaration, no censorship, to start with' (p.76). In the twentieth century, speed became the overarching priority and people grew lazy. They stopped buying and reading books, preferring to access information from digests, tabloids and magazines that delivered their messages in small, bite-sized amounts. Not surprisingly, comic books retained their appeal. The study of the liberal arts fell out of favour; philosophy, history, literature and languages were all dropped from curriculums. By the end of Professor Faber's teaching career, only one student had enrolled in his course on the history of drama. Newspapers died 'like huge moths' (p.115). And the government, seeing the advantages of a culturally illiterate population, 'circled the situation with ... fire-eaters' (p.115).

In this post-literate society, even the conventional understanding of religion has lost its meaning and integrity. Jesus Christ is one of the 'family' now (p.106). The Messiah has been reduced to the level of a game-show host, a saccharine figure beamed out from the ubiquitous parlour walls, spruiking products and entertaining the masses. Faber wonders whether God would recognise his own son 'the way we've dressed him up, or is it dressed him down?' (p.106).

The pursuit of happiness

Key quotes

'So bring on your clubs and parties, your acrobats and magicians, your dare-devils, jet cars, motorcycle helicopters, your sex and heroin, more of everything to do with automatic reflex.' (Beatty, p.80)

'We have everything we need to be happy, but we aren't happy. Something's missing.' (Montag, p.107)

The question of what constitutes happiness is a key concern in *Fahrenheit 451*. Revealingly, one of the first questions that Clarisse asks Montag is in relation to his own happiness and, although he initially resents her boldness, it forces him to be honest with himself and admit that he is not, in fact, happy. In the privileged, hedonistic society depicted in the text, happiness is erroneously equated with fun. By general consensus, having fun is 'everything' (p.85); this is the common goal that swallows up the public's energy, time and headspace. Defined by immediate gratification and diversion, 'fun' consists of activities such as drowning oneself in the 'music and pure cacophony' (p.61) of the televisors, or going to the races or Fun Parks.

People expect, and are expected, to be continually on the move: 'Get people up and running around' (p.83). Everything in this society happens at speed; advertising billboards are now 200 feet long in order to accommodate the fact that people drive past them so fast, so this is the only way commercial messages can be absorbed.

There is an unwritten social contract operating between the government and its citizens. In return for the loss of critical freedoms, such as the right to free speech and intellectual autonomy, people are granted an unlimited licence to play as hard as they please. Indeed, they are encouraged to do so. Beatty argues that the government has fulfilled its obligation to the public by providing as much entertainment as it can digest: 'That's all we live for, isn't it? For pleasure, for titillation?' (p.78). Genuine emotion – such as that felt by Clara Phelps when she listens to

'Dover Beach' – is viewed negatively because it spoils this agenda. Mrs Bowles' reactive fury at Montag's reading reveals a fierce determination to avoid thinking about 'poetry and suicide and crying and awful feelings' (p.131). Even traditional funerals have been eliminated on the basis that they are 'unhappy and pagan' (p.78); there is no space for outpourings of grief, remorse, guilt or any other emotion that might breed discontent.

At the same time, life is cheap, and violence is central to this culture. The government recognises the importance of a safety valve, which alleviates some of the repressed anger that threatens to surface regularly. Parlour games feature brutal, graphic images, with clowns dismembering their companions and cars smashing into bodies. There is unchecked violence in the streets and on the roads. At the fire station, Montag's colleagues torture animals for amusement, baiting the Mechanical Hound and gambling on the result.

In a society that makes a virtue out of selfishness, it is hardly surprising that relationships are profoundly compromised. Intimacy is expendable and romantic love has all but disappeared. The Phelpses are each on their third marriage and describe themselves as 'independent' (p.123), suggesting little emotional investment. The Montags' relationship has been reduced to banal exchanges that highlight their lack of connection. Montag resents continually vying for his wife's attention, stuck in a losing competition with the parlour walls and the Seashells. Neither husband nor wife can even remember when they first met.

The reality is that the hectic, frenzied pace barely disguises an underlying despair. People lead unfulfilled lives that are lacking in joy and purpose. Montag concludes that he is 'a silly empty man' and his wife is 'a silly empty woman' (p.59). Bradbury depicts a society that, beneath the noise, is wretchedly unhappy. Clarisse's rhetorical question – 'Do you notice how people hurt each other nowadays?' (p.42) – goes to the heart of the moral bankruptcy that has seeped into, and now characterises, their lives.

Attempted suicide is so common as to be dismissed as routine by the operators who come to minister to Mildred: 'We get these cases nine or ten a night' (p.24). Abortion is used regularly as a form of birth control, and women elect to have their children by Caesarian section, rather than going through the unpleasant messiness of a natural labour: 'No use going through all that agony for a baby' (p.125). There is little love lost between parents and their children. The young are left to run wild, killing for sport. Clarisse tells Montag that she is frightened of children her own age; a number of her friends have been shot or died in car wrecks. Abandoned by their feckless parents and infected by the general climate of hedonism and self-indulgence, carloads of thrillseeking adolescents drive at high speed during the night in search of adventure. When a shocked Montag barely escapes one such killing spree, he thinks, 'For no reason at all in the world they would have killed me' (p.166).

Key point

Clarisse paints a chilling picture of the prevailing values of society when she reveals, 'everyone I know is either shouting or dancing around like wild or beating up one another' (p.42). Caught up in a frantic whirlpool of pleasure-seeking excess, people are so overstimulated that they do not have the inclination to spend time examining their lives critically.

Conformity and rebellion

Key quotes

'So few want to be rebels any more.' (Faber, p.113)

'I hate a Roman named Status Quo!' (Granger, p.201)

Focused solely on self-gratification, the majority are too busy revelling in the diversions on offer to question the civil liberties they have lost. Yet, arguably, the high suicide rate points to an epidemic of silent mutiny. Even if Mildred is unable to voice her bitter unhappiness, her suicide attempt attests to her unwillingness to continue living life as she knows it.

In the State's mission to create an obedient, homogenous society, equality has taken on a new meaning. It is no longer a question of being born 'free and equal' (p.77). Now everyone must be '*made*' equal (p.77): that is, reduced to the lowest common denominator. If there are no benchmarks of excellence against which to measure themselves, people will be content with shared mediocrity. While books present an obvious danger to this social cohesion – akin to 'a loaded gun in the house next door' (p.77) – there are other threats. Beatty is realistic about mild deviations on the part of his men, recognising that natural curiosity will play its part: 'At least once in his career, every fireman gets an itch. What do the books say, he wonders. Oh, to *scratch* that itch' (p.81).

Beatty is also cynical enough to believe that, even if the firemen do have qualms, they will be too wary to act on them. He understands the importance of fear as a means of control. Not only do people 'always dread the unfamiliar' (p.76), they have good reason to fear the consequences of dissent; it is easier, and safer, to conform. Faber is a typical example. The professor blames himself for being 'one of the innocents who could have spoken up and out when no one would listen to the "guilty", but I did not speak and thus became guilty myself' (p.106). Some of the tactics employed by the State agencies to ensure compliance are decisive and heavy-handed; others are more subtle. Watching the Mechanical Hound toying with its victims is a nightly reminder to Beatty's men of the beast's ruthless efficiency.

Although the 'terrible tyranny of the majority' (p.140) predominates, it does not speak for everyone. The woman who chooses to burn rather than submit to the oppression of the State makes the same moral stand as the sixteenth-century martyrs she quotes. This raid does not follow the usual procedure where the victim's arrest has already occurred. For Montag, the woman's presence spoils the 'ritual' (p.50), and her 'terrible accusing silence' (p.50) does not allow the fireman the luxury of pretending that his actions don't hurt anyone. Reacting with contempt for her persecutors, the woman takes control over her own death by lighting the match that sets the fire.

The old woman's defiance is the catalyst that spurs Montag to act, setting him on his own path of rebellion. Beatty's routine, but belated, homily on their calling has a counterproductive effect, with Montag vowing to himself that he will never return to his old job. Instead, after the chief leaves, Montag starts to read his cache of stolen books. Recognising the immoral state of their society and understanding the part they have all played in its creation is the first critical step towards redemption. Desperate for answers, Montag finds an ally in Faber.

Montag's crude tactic of planting books in the house of a fireman in order to incriminate him is ultimately impractical though, according to Granger, such a strategy might have worked on a national scale. However, memory is a more potent tool of resistance and, collectively, Granger's group has an authority that was lacking when they were separate individuals. They – and others like them – are the custodians of knowledge, memorising facts and ideas formerly contained in books so that they can be passed on to future generations. These men move around the countryside with quiet intent; ironically, they are 'model citizens, in [their] own special way' (p.195).

Key point

Though characters are faced with a corrupt and repressive authority that seeks to rob individuals of their freedom, the novel demonstrates that people can still choose to submit or resist. Moreover, change rests with the individual, and the personal courage and initiative they bring to the task: 'Do your own bit of saving, and if you drown, at least die knowing you were headed for shore' (p.112).

The rise of technology

Key quotes

'A great thunderstorm of sound gushed from the walls ... you had the impression that someone had turned on a washing-machine or sucked you up in a gigantic vacuum.' (pp.60–1)

'Have you ever seen the atom-bomb mushroom from two hundred miles up? It's a pinprick, it's nothing.' (Granger, p.201)

In the world of *Fahrenheit 451*, technology is presented as the seductive alternative to intellectual pursuit, filling the vacuum that has been deliberately created by the destruction of the written word. The government's objective is to create a context in which critical thinking is impossible. Technology is central to this agenda. It is technology in the form of mass media that now provides entertainment and distraction for the population; its lure is addictive and all-consuming.

The novel draws a distinction between the processes of reading and watching. Underpinning Bradbury's scenario is the assumption that reading is a more active experience that allows its audience the wherewithal to ponder and analyse the ideas presented. At the same time – as Faber explains to Montag – it is not so much the absence of books that is problematic, 'it's some of the things that once were in books' (p.107). Faber argues that it would be possible to project 'the same infinite detail and awareness' (p.107) through the current technology – if there was an incentive do so. However, the televisors and the Seashells intentionally pander to the least discerning in the community, bombarding the senses with sound and colour to the exclusion of everything else.

Bradbury's renaming of 'television' to 'televisor' (p.107) is subtle, but effective. Whereas 'television' simply evokes a picture on the screen, 'televisor' is less neutral, implying an advisory, more calculating role. This technology presents a version of the world that simulates reality so convincingly that 'it becomes and is the truth' (p.109). For Mildred, her parlour family is 'real' in a way that characters in books are not, and she finds reading a poor substitute for the excitement of watching her screens. Yet the programs themselves are designed to preclude analysis or discussion, and the televisors promote their messages with absolute conviction in order to discourage doubt: 'It rushes you on so quickly to its own conclusions your mind hasn't time to protest' (p.109). Faber ruefully admits that the ideas contained in books are vulnerable, precisely because they *can* be debated: 'Books can be beaten down with reason. But with all my knowledge and scepticism, I have never been able to argue with a one-hundred-piece symphony orchestra, full colour, three dimensions' (pp.109–10).

Seashells are another insidious tool of the government. These thimble-sized radios, designed to fit snugly in the ear, emit a one-way stream of carefully calibrated information and 'an electronic ocean of sound' (p.20) to a passive recipient. Again, Mildred exemplifies the unquestioning audience targeted by these devices. After ten years of listening to them on a semi-permanent basis, she has become 'an expert at lip-reading' (p.28). Both the parlour walls and the Seashells inhibit, if not eliminate, the opportunity for meaningful discourse. Montag is reminded of the old joke 'about the wife who talked so much on the telephone that her desperate husband ran out to the nearest store and telephoned her to ask what was for dinner' (p.57).

Technology is also deployed in the service of law enforcement. Fugitives from 'justice' are hunted with an array of effective weaponry. Police helicopters turn into beetles when they hit the ground, and then, just as suddenly, return to the air to search for their targets. The Mechanical Hound is a terrifying invention; with eight insect legs and a disproportionate proboscis from which emerges its deadly needle, the Hound exudes malevolence. Its programming is complex and, with a nose so sensitive that it 'can remember and identify ten thousand odour-indexes on ten thousand men without re-setting' (p.172), it is an extraordinarily efficient tracking and killing machine.

The Mechanical Hound embodies the tension between technology and the natural world. A machine that seems to have the personality of a living creature, it 'slept but did not sleep, lived but did not live in its gently humming, gently vibrating, softly illuminated kennel' (p.35). Much of the imagery used to describe it perversely comes from nature: 'It was like a great bee come home from some field where the honey is full of poison wildness' (p.35).

This points to a broader conflict explored in the novel between the natural world and the artificial, fabricated world that has replaced it. The dominance of technology has resulted in people losing touch with nature. This conflict – which is really about values – sees characters such as Clarisse and Granger pitched against those who eschew nature, instead embracing the artifice that is central to their existence. Clarisse's appreciation of the physical world marks her as unusual and, through her, Montag sees his surroundings with fresh eyes. At her suggestion, he looks up at the 'man in the moon' (p.17) and tastes the rain on his tongue. The little gifts that Clarisse leaves on Montag's doorstep are from her garden – flowers, chestnuts, autumn leaves. She often goes out of the city and hikes in the forest, watching birds and collecting butterflies. By contrast, Montag's most significant memory of Mildred is 'of a little girl in a forest without trees' (p.60). Now, the only time his wife drives into the country is when her anger threatens to overwhelm her, and the most pleasurable aspect of the excursion is killing animals at high speed.

Montag's escape to the country triggers a scene from his childhood: a rare day when he visited a farm. He now imagines spending a night in a barn full of fresh hay, listening to the sounds around him and smelling the warm rural air. The countryside is presented as an authentic experience, as opposed to the 'seven veils of unreality' and the parlour walls of the city (p.182). This pastoral utopia will nourish Montag, and protect him from the 'sound of death' (p.183) coming from the sky. Significantly, the memory of Clarisse is entwined with this fantasy.

Granger argues that people cannot afford to ignore the wilderness as it is ultimately more powerful than the human-made world. Quoting his grandfather, he emphasises the importance of respecting the environment and understanding humanity's place within it. Nature can 'take back what it has given, as easily as blowing its breath on us or sending the sea to tell us we are not so big' (p.201). As it happens, events in *Fahrenheit 451* show how humankind's own capacity for self-destruction can assist this process, colluding with nature by making use of the danger it poses. Technology can turn on its creators – the atomic bombs that wipe out Montag's city at the end of the text represent technology at its most lethal – allowing the wilderness to reclaim the upper hand.

DIFFERENT INTERPRETATIONS

Different interpretations arise from different responses to a text. Over time, a text will evoke a wide range of responses from its readers, who may come from various social or cultural groups and live in very different places and historical periods. Responses by critics and reviewers can be published in newspapers, journals and books, both online and in print. They can also be expressed in discussions among readers in the media, classrooms, book groups and so on.

While there is no single correct reading or interpretation of a text, it is important to understand that an interpretation is more than a personal opinion – it is the justification of a point of view on a text. To present an interpretation of a text based on your point of view, you must use a logical argument and support it with relevant evidence from the text.

Critical viewpoints

Fahrenheit 451 has continued to excite critics and audiences since its original publication in 1953. In an obituary published in *The New York Times*, Gerald Jonas suggests that, by many estimates, Bradbury 'was the writer most responsible for bringing modern science fiction into the literary mainstream' (Jonas 2012). Jonas calls Bradbury a master whose 'imaginative and lyrical evocations of the future reflected both the optimism and the anxieties of his own post-war America'. The novel has been read as a critique of government oppression, an attack on mass culture and 'an elitist fantasy in which the ignorance of the masses leads to their inevitable destruction and the ruling class then assumes its rightful place as the guardians of culture' (Enns 2015). Sam Weller, Bradbury's authorised biographer, attests to the author's own shifting and, at times, contradictory explanations as to what the book is about (Weller 2018).

Reviewers have been unanimous in their praise for the novel's prescience and continued relevance. Writing for *The Guardian*, Sam Jordison argues that, after more than fifty years, the central message of *Fahrenheit 451* still resonates: 'the most enduring books often take a while to seep into the popular consciousness' (Jordison 2008). Heidi Hammel, in *The New York Times*, observes that Bradbury accurately predicted societal, as well as technological, change, stating that 'Bradbury's exploration of the future of society intuited that the burgeoning "many" would lead to isolating disconnect for the individual' (Hammel 2015). In a similar vein, Rahim Bahrani, the director of the HBO film version of *Fahrenheit 451*, calls it 'the book for our social media age' (Bahrani 2018).

There have been a few caveats. Bradbury has been accused of being too didactic. Yet, if large sections of the novel seem 'preachy', its language is also 'often startling and poetic' and 'almost as memorable for its images as its ideas' (Jordison 2008). In an interesting essay for *The Arts Fuse*, Patrick Pritchett contends that there is a fundamental paradox underpinning *Fahrenheit 451*: 'It never occurs to Ray Bradbury that, by just championing the great works of Western civilization and consigning pop culture (notably science-fiction) to the flames, he's exercising his own pernicious brand of censorship' (Pritchett 2018). Pritchett is also critical of the gendering of middle-brow culture – 'TV is for anesthetising women, and not a proper activity for virile men' – insisting that this is one of the 'more deplorably dated' aspects of the book.

These responses highlight the different ways in which readers can respond to elements of any given text.

Two interpretations

Interpretation 1: In *Fahrenheit 451*, the characters have little control over their fates.

The destinies of the vast majority living in the dystopian future envisaged by Bradbury are shaped much more by the State than by self-determination. The repressive political climate is the key reason why individuals have so little personal autonomy, but there are also variables such as gender and cultural expectations at play. In this context, destinies are controlled by prevailing powerbrokers and random events.

In the text, individual rights and freedoms are less important than the interests of the State. Although the US is a hedonistic society, people are denied intellectual liberty. Books are banned, and any form of dissent is brutally supressed. People suspected of deviating from the status quo – such as the McClellans – are kept under surveillance; no one who breaks the law is safe. Ominously, the community has essentially become self-monitoring, which means that people cannot trust their friends or neighbours. The woman who burns is denounced by her neighbour, Mrs Blake, who rings in her suspicions to the station. Mildred and her friends inform on Montag. With this kind of complicity from a self-serving public, there is increasingly less need for the firemen; they simply have to 'provide a circus now and then ... to keep things in line' (p.113). If the social equilibrium is threatened, the terrifying spectre of the Mechanical Hound is deployed to restore public order. Moreover, as the manhunt for Montag shows, the Hound can be capricious in its choice of victim.

In this society, power is invested exclusively in men; politics, policing and the professions are all male domains. Montag's own vocation has been decided by patriarchal tradition. He insists to Mildred, 'My grandfather and father were firemen. In my sleep, I ran after them' (p.68). By contrast, women's roles are confined to a narrow domestic arena. Mildred and her friends lead aimless, vacuous lives, devoted to their parlour walls and the anodyne socialising deemed acceptable by the authorities. Despite the unrelenting emphasis on '*fun*' (p.113), many feel trapped and unhappy; for some, suicide is the only way out.

Montag is determined to strike out on his own. However, he acts reflexively. At first, he does not even acknowledge breaking the law, stealing books ostensibly without conscious choice: 'Montag had done nothing. His hand had done it all ... with a brain of its own' (p.51).

He is simply carried along by events, responding to situations as they arise, without regard for the consequences. After murdering Beatty, he chastises himself for his recklessness: 'you're a fool, a damn fool ... look at the mess, and what do you do?' (p.157).

Moreover, there are millions who live in fear or indifference, passively accepting their fate. Montag condemns the unwillingness of his fellow Americans to confront the delusions with which they live, instead eating 'shadows for breakfast and steam for lunch and vapours for supper' (p.180). Although Faber deplores the direction society has taken, he is reluctant to place himself at risk: 'Why waste your final hours racing about your cage denying you're a squirrel?' (p.114). Had Montag not approached him, the old professor would have lived out his days in silent regret.

Like Faber, Granger and his friends – all eminent academics in their fields – have fallen victim to the new regime, losing their positions and their livelihoods. Either their university departments changed hands, or their fields became obsolete; for example, ethics is now an 'ancient study' (p.192). Reverend Padover abruptly lost his congregation after expressing politically incorrect views. Interestingly, Granger wrote a book delineating the 'proper' relationship between the individual and society. This presumably explored the very checks and balances that are conspicuously absent in the prevailing dictatorship that has seen these men persecuted.

Life in Bradbury's reimagined US is full of random acts of violence and arbitrary cruelty. Fun has a deadly edge. When Montag is fleeing the police, he is deliberately targeted and nearly killed by a carload of lethally exuberant teenagers who are speeding down a suburban street. These joy rides are a regular occurrence, often resulting in the deaths of hapless pedestrians or of the teenagers themselves. Montag wonders if Clarisse might have been one of their victims. Certainly, many of her friends have died in similar circumstances: 'I'm afraid of children my own age. They kill each other' (p.42).

America's political dominance and global aggression has meant suffering for the rest of the world; the country's wealth presents a stark contrast to the poverty endemic elsewhere. Despised and feared, America now lives under siege. When the long-awaited war arrives, it is catastrophic, annihilating whole cities across the country in seconds. Millions perish, anonymous casualties whose fate is decided by their political masters. One of these is Mildred, who dies in a hotel room surrounded by the 'great shimmering walls of colour and motion' (p.203) – the 'family' on whom she is so reliant cannot save her from oblivion. The few who do survive, including Granger's little band, are left with nothing but their memories and the uncertain hope of a better future.

Fahrenheit 451 highlights how irrelevant self-determination is for the majority in Bradbury's dystopia. The broader political and social context defines the way in which individual lives – and deaths – are played out. Irrespective of strength of will or desire, these characters have little control over their fate.

Interpretation 2: *Fahrenheit 451* demonstrates that individuals can control their own fates.

Faber tells Montag, 'We all have our harps to play. And it's up to you now to know with which ear you'll listen' (p.140). He is speaking from his own experience. Although *Fahrenheit 451* acknowledges the repressive political and social context that governs people's lives, it suggests that individuals still have agency and are largely responsible for their own destinies. They can live in apathy, submissively accepting a corrupt status quo, or they can empower themselves by rebelling against it.

The American people live under a totalitarian regime but, arguably, they have colluded in their own oppression by virtue of the choices they have made. They have entered into an unholy trade-off with the government where, in exchange for the permission to pursue pleasure with impunity, they have relinquished their intellectual freedom. The trend to a post-literate, post-truth society began with the people. They gave up reading voluntarily, long before books were officially demonised, paving the way for the government to capitalise on the development. Faber frames the current state of their society as a deliberate choice: 'After all, when we *had* all the books we needed, we still insisted on finding the highest cliff to jump off' (p.111). This view is echoed by Beatty when he says, 'People want to be happy ... Don't we keep them moving, don't we give them fun?' (p.78). The majority would prefer not to think about anything that interferes with this priority – hence Mrs Bowles' anger over the 'mush' (p.131) contained in 'Dover Beach'.

In general, people show little interest in the governing politics that might make a difference to their lives. Although Mrs Bowles votes – 'same as everyone' (p.125) – she is deaf to the actual message of the respective parties. To Montag's frustration, she has no idea what the presidential candidates had to say and her vote is based entirely on their appearance. As far as Mildred and her friends are concerned, the present incumbent, Winston Noble, has all the right qualifications for leadership: an impressive name and the distinction of being 'one of the nicest-looking men' (p.125) in political history. In this sense, the electorate gets the government it deserves. Montag rages against the inertia of Mildred's friends, but his anger is also directed at everyone who allowed the current situation to prevail, including himself: 'Go home and think about how it all happened and what did you ever do to stop it?' (p.131).

Nevertheless, there are characters in the text who reject being told how to think or what to read. Faber is an interesting example in that, initially, he typifies the passive response of the public. By his own admission, he did nothing when he might have made a difference. However, he makes a conscious decision to trust Montag after their first conversation in the park. The old professor has never entirely given up hope that things might change. He has built his audio-capsule in the hope that one day the right person will approach him and his device might be used to build support: 'In silence, our stage-whisper might carry' (p.116). Similarly, the McClellans do not endorse their society's values. Encouraged by her family, and her uncle in particular, Clarisse has formulated her own ideas with regard to the cultural mayhem that surrounds her. Despite the constraints imposed by the overarching context, these individuals maintain their integrity and their principles by refusing to conform.

Even those who are actively persecuted by the State retain the right to self-determination. Like the Reformation martyrs whose example she quotes, the woman who burns with her books chooses to die, rather than recant or be imprisoned. She also decides the manner of her death, striking the match that will set the blaze. Equally, Beatty choses his own fate, provocatively goading Montag into killing him: 'Beatty had wanted to die. He had just stood there, not really trying to save himself' (p.158).

As a fireman, Montag is an integral part of this system, yet he is able to reject its values. When he starts to question his own role, he realises how corruptible his society is and how flawed his relationships are. The recognition that the people he knows and regards are either dying or already dead informs his determination to make a stand: 'That's the good part of dying; when you've got nothing to lose, you run any risk you want' (p.110). While Montag's stance is an explosive one, spanning a mere few days, Granger and his band are more discreet rebels. Having lost their positions, they could have simply accepted the hand they were dealt, like Faber. Instead, they take to the road – 'crackpots with verses in their heads' (p.197) – unobtrusively ensuring that the books are on file 'behind their quiet eyes' (p.198) for when better times arrive.

Change begins with individuals such as these. Granger's conviction that humanity – like the Phoenix – is able to resurrect itself and, by implication, make less destructive choices in the future suggests that people *can* control their own destinies. *Fahrenheit 451* shows that a just and enlightened society is contingent on making the right societal choices, and acts as a warning about the consequences of making the wrong ones. The result is a world defined by tyranny and selfishness. However, with the value of hindsight, people *could* do things differently; it is in their hands.

QUESTIONS & ANSWERS

This section focuses on your own analytical writing on the text, and gives you strategies for producing high quality responses in your coursework and exam essays.

Essay writing – an overview

An essay on a literary work is a formal and serious piece of writing that presents your point of view on the text, usually in response to a given topic. Your 'point of view' in an essay is your interpretation of the meaning of the text's language, structure, characters, situations and events, supported by detailed analysis of textual evidence.

Analyse – don't summarise

In your essays it is important to avoid simply summarising what happens in a text.

- A **summary** is a description or paraphrase (retelling in different words) of the characters and events. For example: 'Macbeth has a horrifying vision of a dagger dripping with blood before he goes to murder King Duncan.'
- An **analysis** is an explanation of the real meaning or significance that lies 'beneath' the text's words (and images, for a film). For example: 'Macbeth's vision of a bloody dagger shows how deeply uneasy he is about the violent act he is contemplating, and conveys his sense that supernatural forces are impelling him to act.'

A limited amount of summary is sometimes necessary to let your reader know which part of the text you wish to discuss. However, always keep this to a minimum and follow it immediately with your analysis of what this part of the text is really telling us.

Plan your essay

Carefully plan your essay so that you have a clear idea of what you are going to say. The plan ensures that your ideas flow logically, that your argument remains consistent and that you stay on the topic. An essay plan should be a list of **brief dot points** covering no more than half a page.

- Include your central argument or main contention – a concise statement of your overall response to the topic.
- Write three or four dot points for each paragraph, indicating the main idea and evidence/examples from the text. Note that in your essay you will need to *expand* on these points and *analyse* the evidence.

Structure your essay

An essay is a complete, self-contained piece of writing. It has a clear beginning (the introduction), middle (several body paragraphs) and end (the last paragraph or conclusion). It must also have a central argument that runs throughout, linking each paragraph to form a coherent whole. See examples of introductions and conclusions in the 'Analysing a sample topic' and 'Sample answer' sections.

The introduction establishes your overall response to the topic. It includes your main contention and outlines the main evidence you will refer to in the course of the essay. Write your introduction *after* you have done a plan and *before* you write the rest of the essay.

The body paragraphs argue your case – they present evidence from the text and explain how this evidence supports your argument. Each body paragraph needs:

- a strong **topic sentence** (usually the first sentence) that states the main point being made in the paragraph
- **evidence** from the text, including some brief quotations
- **analysis** of the textual evidence, with **explanation** of its significance and how it supports your argument
- **links back to the topic** in one or more statements, usually towards the end of the paragraph.

Connect the body paragraphs so that your discussion flows smoothly. Use some linking words and phrases such as 'similarly' and 'on the other hand', though don't start every paragraph like this. Another strategy is to use a significant word from the last sentence of one paragraph in the first sentence of the next.

Use key terms from the topic – or synonyms for them – throughout, so the relevance of your discussion to the topic is always clear.

The conclusion ties everything together and finishes the essay. It includes strong statements that emphasise your central argument and provide a clear response to the topic.

Avoid simply restating the points made earlier in the essay – this will end on a very flat note and imply that you have run out of ideas and vocabulary. The conclusion should be a logical extension of what you have written, not just a repetition or summary of it. Writing an effective conclusion can be a challenge. Try using these tips:

- Start by linking back to the final sentence of the second-last paragraph, rather than leaping to your main contention straight away – this helps your writing to flow.
- Use synonyms and expressions with equivalent meanings to vary your vocabulary. This allows you to reinforce your line of argument without being repetitive.
- When planning your essay, think of one or two broad statements or observations about the text's wider meaning. These should be related to the topic and your overall argument. Keep them for the conclusion, since they will give you something 'new' to say but still follow logically from your discussion. The introduction will be focused on the topic, but the conclusion can present a wider view of the text.

Essay topics

1. "Nobody listens anymore." How important is communication in the society of *Fahrenheit 451*?
2. 'The characters in *Fahrenheit 451* are motivated more by fear than by anything else.' Do you agree?
3. "We all made the right kind of mistakes, or we wouldn't be here." Does Montag always make the right mistakes?
4. "Those who don't build must burn."
   Does the novel show this to be true?
5. 'In *Fahrenheit 451*, Bradbury depicts a world that is both cruel and full of contradictions.' Discuss.
6. How does the novel explore the concept of personal freedom?
7. 'Although Montag becomes increasingly rash, the reader does not lose sympathy for him.' Do you agree?
8. '*Fahrenheit 451* puts its message above everything else.'
   To what extent do you agree?
9. 'In what is essentially a story of rebellion, Bradbury maintains a constant tension between bleak cynicism and hope.' Discuss.
10. 'Regardless of their social position, the characters in *Fahrenheit 451* feel powerless.' To what extent do you agree?

Vocabulary for writing on *Fahrenheit 451*

Allegory: a story with a meaning or message other than the literal one – the text invites interpretation on at least two levels.

Dystopian: a narrative that explores an imaginary society in which there is great injustice and cruelty.

Intertextuality: the deliberate referencing of other texts within a text – either directly, by allusion or quotation, or indirectly by paraphrase or imitation.

Linear structure: a narrative that presents events in chronological order.

Motif: a recurring image used to link ideas and reinforce themes; adds cohesion and unity to the writing.

Patriarchy: a society in which all the power structures – political, religious, legal and domestic – are invested in men.

Third-person limited: a variation on the omniscient (all-seeing, all-knowing) narrator, this third-person narrative point of view is limited to one character's perspective.

Totalitarian: a form of government that is repressive and dictatorial, requiring complete subservience to the State.

Analysing a sample topic

"Those who don't build must burn." Does the novel show this to be true?

This question focuses on the kind of society depicted in the novel. What are the prevailing values underpinning American society, and how do these inform the actions of the various characters? You are asked a direct question here – you must answer it. Make your contention clear in the introduction and indicate your line of argument.

The topic is a thematic one that requires you to look across the whole text. First, identify the topic quotation and consider the context in which it appears (p.116). Then consider individual characters and determine whether they fit easily into one category or the other (i.e. building or burning). Note the 'must' in the quote. How much coercion is there in this society? How inevitable is its demise? Avoid adopting too rigid a position. It is often difficult to substantiate 'black-and-white' responses, which can fail to acknowledge the complexity implicit in the question.

The following plan is only one way to tackle the question. For example, you could place more emphasis on the macro level, exploring the implications of the government's international aggression.

Sample introduction

Professor Faber claims that 'those who don't build must burn', suggesting that people either contribute to their society in a productive way, or they destroy it. This stark dichotomy is borne out – at a personal, as well as societal level – in the dystopian world of Ray Bradbury's *Fahrenheit 451*. The United States of the future no longer values creating or learning; instead, destruction is elevated to a rarefied level. Scholarship is maligned and books, as the tangible symbols of knowledge, are literally burned. The novel demonstrates that, ultimately, everyone must make a choice to build or to burn – or the choice will be made for them.

Body paragraph outline

Paragraph 1: The US has changed beyond recognition from the nation of builders it once was.

- The US is a dangerous presence in the world, having initiated and won two atomic wars 'since 1960' (p.96).
- Domestically, the entrepreneurial energy that once made the country great has been channelled exclusively into policing and the entertainment sector.
- The priority is now the feckless pursuit of pleasure, much of which has a destructive, violent edge.
- Those who once worked in education and expressed creative ideas, such as Granger and his fellow academics, have been disgraced and exiled.
- Mildred and her friends exemplify the lifestyle of most Americans: they lead a parasitical existence, making no real contribution to society.

Paragraph 2: The weaponisation of fire underpins this inherently destructive culture.

- The firemen are the formidable, frontline representatives of an autocratic regime that destroys books, cultural icons, houses, libraries and even lives.
- Note Beatty's casual indifference to the familiar pattern of the 'fanatics' who 'always try suicide' (p.53).
- All houses are equipped with wall-incinerators: 'A problem gets too burdensome, then into the furnace with it' (p.150).
- Montag realises that his only contribution to the city has been 'ashes' (p.200). If he and the other firemen continue to burn – even as the sun 'burned Time' (p.181) – then there will be literally nothing left.

Paragraph 3: At the same time, the novel takes a nuanced approach, and there are individuals who are more difficult to categorise.

- Some characters come to a belated realisation that their lives need to change; others never get the chance, irrespective of their good intentions.
- Look at Clarisse and her family, or the woman who burns with her books. These individuals want to 'build' a more constructive society, but end up casualties of more powerful forces.
- There are also those who sit on the fence – such as Faber – unwilling to commit either way. Whether they are motivated by fear, apathy or self-interest, they find it easier to avoid conflict.

Paragraph 4: Bradbury's morality tale emphasises the cyclical nature of humanity's struggle.

- Retribution awaits the characters who have allied themselves with the government; for example, Beatty is burned to death by Montag.
- On a larger scale, an atomic inferno reduces the city to ashes.
- Humanity's salvation will come from the few who have rejected prevailing values.

→

- Granger has been inspired by the generous example of his grandfather, who was a sculptor, a musician and a philanthropist: 'The world was bankrupted of ten million fine actions the night he passed on' (p.200).
- In this spirit, Granger and his fellow survivors retain knowledge until the world is ready to use it again.
- Note the symbolism of the Phoenix: 'some day we'll stop making the goddam funeral pyres and jumping into the middle of them' (p.209).

Sample conclusion

Granger has been taught by his grandfather that people should make their mark on the world in a positive way: 'Everyone must leave something behind when he dies' (p.200). However, in *Fahrenheit 451*, true builders are conspicuous by their absence. Values such as creativity, service and legacy are foreign to this culture. Rather, the US has embraced a destructive ethos that ultimately precipitates its own destruction. When the wheel comes full circle, those who refuse to build do, indeed, end up paying the price.

SAMPLE ANSWER

"Nobody listens anymore." How important is communication in the society of *Fahrenheit 451*?

Communication is a highly prized commodity in Ray Bradbury's futuristic novel *Fahrenheit 451*. The caveat is that communication is defined and perceived differently, depending on who is interacting with whom. To the government, communication is a one-way street, synonymous with propaganda. Uncensored communication is considered dangerous, potentially subversive. However, to characters such as Clarisse, Faber and Granger, the reciprocal exchange of ideas with other people signifies the first step towards freedom.

It is precisely because the government recognises the importance of communication that it seeks to control the flow of information. It does this through repressive social policies and by controlling mass media. Thus, it effectively creates a cultural context in which the State's voice dominates, and its messages are the only thing that is heard. With the formal banning of books, the ideas contained in them are stifled. History can then be rewritten so that it supports the current narrative. For example, using a half-truth to obfuscate the past, Benjamin Franklin is recast as the first fireman to burn 'English-influenced books in the Colonies', thus framing his initiative as an act of patriotism. Given the government's policy of discrediting as much of the written word as possible, it is ironic that Beatty reaches for the firemen's rule-book to validate this version of history.

Indeed, Beatty's evangelical monologues exemplify the one-sided nature of the communication championed by the government. As one of its spokesmen, the fire chief is perversely well read, articulate and persuasive. He is also utterly dismissive of the merit of books, deeming them irrelevant and contradictory: 'What traitors books can be! You think they're backing you up, and they turn on you.' The policies Beatty represents have reinforced people's contempt for reading.

This contempt has fed into the education system, which has been misappropriated in the interests of the State, its independence and academic credibility lost. Schools and universities offer a selective curriculum that deliberately avoids the humanities, with literacy standards downgraded to the most basic levels: 'Why learn anything save pressing buttons, pulling switches, fitting nuts and bolts?' Teaching is didactic and centred on a screen; enquiry-based learning is denounced. Furthermore, everything that encouraged spontaneous discourse in the past has been eradicated. Even front porches have been stripped from contemporary housing design, to discourage the wrong sort of socialising: 'People talked too much. And they had time to think.'

Equally, the government maintains tight controls on what the public accesses by way of entertainment. Beguiling alternatives, such as the Fun Parks and the races, keep people on the move: 'Life is immediate, the job counts, pleasure lies all about after work.' The televisors and Seashell radios are expedient distractions, essentially designed to prevent people from communicating with one another. Passive immersion in the parlour games, or listening to the Seashells, does not encourage the same reciprocity as reading a book or talking to a friend.

As such, Montag feels a stranger in his own home and finds it impossible to communicate with his wife: 'Well, wasn't there a wall between him and Mildred, when you came down to it. Literally not just one wall but, so far, three!' Mildred's emotional investment in her parlour relatives dominates their relationship. She deludes herself that there is a personal connection with 'the gibbering pack of tree-apes that said nothing, nothing, nothing and said it loud, loud, loud', whereas she is simply part of an anonymous audience interacting with a standardised program. The parlour walls are designed in such a way as to engender a false sense of intimacy, with the client's name automatically supplied by a converter attachment. Montag challenges Mildred's dependence on her 'family' and the other characters whose presence she craves: 'Does the White Clown love you?'

In this way, the screen has become a substitute for meaningful interaction. In one sense, Mildred is avid for the company of her friends. When the front door announces the arrival of Mrs Phelps and Mrs Bowles, she runs from the parlour to greet them 'like a native fleeing an eruption of Vesuvius'. However, the three women then retreat into 'the volcano's mouth' where they have to scream at each other over the manic din created by the televisors. Montag's attempt to engage them in conversation, after turning off the program, is an abject failure: 'Their faces grew haunted with silence.'

Montag's acute sense of alienation is what triggers his search for answers, telling Faber in despair that 'nobody listens anymore'. Naively, he hopes that books may be able to help him understand why their society is in 'such a mess', but the professor explains that books were 'only one type of receptacle where we stored a lot of things we were afraid we might forget'. While books do not have a monopoly on communicating ideas, mass media in the current context has no interest in doing so.

Finding like-minded people with whom he can communicate honestly is the beginning of Montag's journey. Clarisse is the first, complimenting the fireman on his unusual receptiveness: 'When I talk, you look at me.' Those characters who refuse to relinquish their intellectual independence are a direct and dynamic challenge to the inertia of the majority. The closed spaces that feature in the text – claustrophobic interiors such as the 'family' room, Mildred's bedroom and the firehouse clubroom – reinforce the sense of an oppressive, insular society that stifles freedom of expression. It is no accident, therefore, that Montag meets the people who invite transparency and expose him to new ways of thinking, outside. These open spaces – the street where Montag talks with Clarisse, the green park where he meets Faber, the country landscape where he encounters Granger and his band of insurgents – expand exponentially as Montag's resistance grows stronger.

When Montag meets the group who will become his new family, he recognises that it is not only the fire around which they sit that is different – it is also the 'special silence'. The absence of noise creates a welcome space where there is time to reflect and converse; the voices 'were turning the world over and looking at it'. Granger understands that communication cannot be rushed, pointing out that 'you can't make people listen'; they 'have to come round in their own time'.

Fahrenheit 451 explores a world in which truth is deliberately manipulated by a government intent on ensuring compliance and homogeneity. Communication between the State and the people involves promulgating a web of lies and misinformation. At the same time, the text shows that genuine communication is the pathway to a more open, democratic society. Individuals who are able to listen and share ideas without censure will be part of this better future.

REFERENCES & READING

Text

Bradbury, R 2008, *Fahrenheit 451*, HarperCollins, London. First published in 1953.

References and further reading

Bahrani, R 2018, 'Why *Fahrenheit 451* is the Book for Our Social Media Age', *The New York Times Book Review*, 10 May, https://www.nytimes.com/2018/05/10/books/review/fahrenheit-451-ray-bradbury.html

Enns, A 2015, 'The Poet of the Pulps: Ray Bradbury and the Struggle for Prestige in Postwar Science Fiction', *Belphegor*, 13 January, https://journals.openedition.org/belphegor/615

Flock, E 2011, '*Fahrenheit 451*, 50 Years Later, Still Sharply Divides Readers over Ray Bradbury', *The Washington Post*, 26 August, https://www.washingtonpost.com/blogs/blogpost/post/fahrenheit-451-50-years-later-still-sharply-divides-readers-over-ray-bradbury/2011/08/26/gIQAn596fJ_blog.html

Hammel, H 2015, '*Fahrenheit 451* by Ray Bradbury', *The New York Times*, 29 December, https://www.nytimes.com/roomfordebate/2015/12/29/what-science-fiction-movie-or-novel-is-most-prescient-today/fahrenheit-451-by-ray-bradbury

Jonas, Gerald 2012, 'Ray Bradbury, Who Brought Mars to Earth with a Lyrical Mastery, Dies at 91', *The New York Times*, 6 June, https://nytimes.com/2012/06/07/books/ray-bradbury-popularizer-of-science-fiction-dies-at-91.html

Jordison, S 2008, 'Burning Still: *Fahrenheit 451*', *The Guardian*, 16 January, https://www.theguardian.com/books/booksblog/2008/jan/15/burningstillfahrenheit451

Orwell, G 2008, *Nineteen Eighty-Four*, Penguin, London. First published in 1949.

Pritchett, P 2018, '*Fahrenheit 451* and Cultural Betrayal', *The Arts Fuse*, 14 June, https://artsfuse.org/171185/book-commentary-fahrenheit-451-and-cultural-betrayal/

Weller, S 2018, 'Did Ray Bradbury Do a 180 on *Fahrenheit 451*?', *The Dallas Morning News*, 8 November, https://www.dallasnews.com/arts-entertainment/books/2018/11/08/did-ray-bradbury-do-a-180-on-fahrenheit-451/

Films

Fahrenheit 451 1966, dir. François Truffaut, Universal Pictures. Starring Julie Christie, Oskar Werner and Cyril Cusack.

Fahrenheit 451 2018, dir. Ramin Bahrani, HBO Films. Starring Michael B Jordan, Michael Shannon and Sophia Boutella.